THE MASTER COURSE™

THE MASTER COURSE™

YOU CAN HAVE IT ALL!

JL SCOTT

Transitions Publishing Company

Copyright © 2002-2014 Transitions Publishing Company
Softback Edition Copyright © 2015

The moral right of the author has been asserted.

All rights reserved.
No part of this publication may be reproduced, stored in a retrieval system, or transmitted, in any form or by any means, without the prior permission in writing of the publisher, nor be otherwise circulated in any form of binding or cover other than that in which it is published and without a similar condition including this condition being imposed on the subsequent purchaser.

Published by Transitions Publishing Company

ISBN 978-0-692-47828-8

Cover design by Odyssey Books

Typesetting services by BOOKOW.COM

To Duke
My Teacher
My Mentor
My Eternal Friend

Contents

Transform Your Life	1
I **Part One**	5
Successful Creation	7
Creative Techniques	10
Deprivation-Consciousness	13
Positive Mind-Sets ...	15
Signs of Land	17
Your Health - Your Wealth Your Happiness	20
Principles of Transformation	21
Universal Principles	25
Principle of Oneness	32
Replacing Attitudes & Beliefs	36
Change of Perception	40
Prosperity and Wealth	42
Let It Go	46
If the Desire Is Yours the Manifestation Is Yours	49
Health, Youth & Physical Well-Being	52
Mind/Body Control	55
Everything Works Both Ways	59
"Death Talk"	61
Cell Response	64

Fulfilling Relationships	67
Choosing Intimate Relationships	69
Creating Your Fulfilling Relationship	74
Recognizing the Real Thing	78
The Road to Transformation	81
Physical Consciousness	82
Psychic Consciousness	84
Spiritual Consciousness	86
Moving Forward	88

II Part Two — 91

Introduction to Part Two	93
Yes, But ...	95
Living With Fear	97
A Matter of Resistance	99
Building Commitment	101
The Power of Silence	103
Keeping Quiet	105
Energy of Life	107
Prosperity and Wealth	110
Mental Consciousness	112
Remember Who You Are	114
Fear of Economic Insecurity	116
Is It Selfish?	119
The First Step to Wealth	121
Creating a Void	122
Physical Well-Being	127
Cell Relationships	130
Herbs & Vitamins	135

	Aroma Therapy	137
	Intimate Relationships	140
	Infatuation vs. Love	143
	Deciding What It Takes	146
	Personality Characteristics	148
	Expectations	150
	Doing the Groundwork	152
III	**Part Three**	**155**
	Introduction to Part Three	157
	Universal Laws	160
	Start at the Beginning	163
	Getting What You Want	166
	Making Choices	172
	Affirmations	177
	Beliefs About Wealth	179
	Choosing Wealth	182
	Stressing Your Health	186
	A Short Story	191
	Choosing Health	195
	Balance & Control	200
	What Is True Love?	202
	Choosing Intimacy	206
	Are You Ready?	211
	The Priority	214
	Heading Off "Failure"	215
IV	**Part Four**	**221**
	Introduction to Part Four	223

Ready to Begin	225
Letting Go	226
Create Your Space	228
Open Your Mind	230
Creative Energy	231
Perspective on Fear	233
Still, Small Voice	235
Basic Creation	237
General Tips for Creating	238
Creating Wealth	242
Creating Health & Anti-Aging	253
Creating Your Relationship	262
Waiting For Your Creation	269
Additional Tips	271
The Master's Path	276
Who, Or What, Is Running Your Life?	283
Additional Resource	285
V Appendix	**287**
Self-Analysis Guide	289
Directions	293
Questionnaire	296
Making Life Experiences Work!	302
Changing Core Belief Feelings	304
Reaching Your Goal	313
Relaxation	315
VI Epilogue	**321**

Transform Your Life

A Special Message from the Author

I wrote *The MASTER COURSE* after years of facilitating seminars, teaching workshops and counseling people who wanted to create lives full of success and joy. This experience taught me every desire for happiness is based in one of three areas of life: *physical well-being - financial success and security - and relationships of all types.*

The caterpillar becomes a butterfly. Did you ever hear of a butterfly changing back into a caterpillar? Of course not! It's the secret of transformation rather than "change."

Self-help success techniques - often bring temporary change. But, they don't work over the long haul! Positive thinking/mental attitude - affirmations - creative visualization – meditation: All great processes! All will bring about change. Yet, rarely does the change last indefinitely.

Change is not the answer! The only thing certain about change is that it's temporary. Transformation, on the other hand, is complete. The butterfly never changes back into a caterpillar.

Everything in this Course is related to the universal principles behind our creative processes. Without full knowledge, understanding, and use of these underlying principles, even change loses its power and never becomes permanent. This information has been gathered from many sources, over many years! Some even came through my own brain – although, I do *not* call it channeling!

Do you fit into any of the following groups?

- You have been trying for years to create change in your life only to see it float away - just when you think you've got it. You've begun to think all that "positive thinking" is nonsense. Not to mention the other processes you may have tried. Yet, you're willing to try it one more time - with the principles that will let you keep what you accomplish.

- You have used life creation techniques and they have worked wonderfully in a particular area of your life. Yet, you can't seem to get those same techniques to work in other areas. For instance, maybe you have gained control over your finances but can't really enjoy it because you're still suffering from poor health. Or, perhaps you've taken control over your physical well being - but you're still alone - unable to find a satisfying relationship.

- You are new to the "creating your own life" process. And, you want to get the ultimate instruction - the first time - without the discouraging experience of watching your life change for the better - only to see it all fall apart just when you think you're winning.

- You have tried several internet marketing projects with just so-so results. Or, maybe you're in business for yourself. You want to know how to make every project you launch a huge success - with tremendous ongoing income. (I mention this one because since I decided to use the internet as a publishing medium, I've become aware of the thousands of people trying one money-making project after another - with disappointingly low results.)

"If nothing changes – nothing changes"

Would you like to see real Life Transformation - rather than just temporary change that could reverse itself at any minute? I mean transformation in all areas of your life. If so, use this Course in depth. Study it - learn it - live it. It will teach you the universal principles - as well as the necessary mind-sets - for successful life transformation.

The first four chapters of Part One contain necessary information for creation in every part of your life. The next three chapters will give more specific information regarding financial prosperity - physical well-being - and relationships. The final chapter will give you a road map showing you the path to your final destination. Transformation!

Part One of *The MASTER COURSE* aims at helping you adjust your thought processes and mind-sets. You'll find some simple action techniques to assist you to that end. You will also benefit from thoroughly thinking through the ideas presented here.

Part One is the foundation of the Course! Read it - then re-read it - as often as you can over the next 30 days. Let the ideas sink in firmly. Begin to get into the habit of actually doing the action techniques. They will grow more complicated later. Right now, we're setting up new habit patterns.

Part Two through Part Four will give you additional details for transformation in all three major areas of life. They also contain specific - and more detailed - action techniques along with additional resources to help you toward your goal.

The MASTER COURSE is designed to take you through all the necessary steps to transformation. Each Parts' lessons *must* be thoroughly internalized. Try to be patient and know this is the best way for you to achieve *lasting change.*

Always remember: you didn't get where you are overnight. Learning conscious control of your life will also take some time.

Nothing has been presented in this book I haven't either experienced myself – or seen others create. Some things are more important than others to different people. Whatever you wish to create *must* be important to you.

I have been driven to find answers for my entire life, and I have written this course over many years. I have gathered information from many sources in my own search for a life plan. Finally, I have chosen what works over and over and over.

In the Appendix of this book, you will find *The MASTER COURSE* Workbook, *"Who's Driving Your Bus?"* The Workbook will help you work through any unconscious beliefs that may be standing in the way of you creating the life you've always wanted.

This Self-Analysis Guide is your personal research guide to your own unconscious mind. You'll be amazed when you find the true reasons behind what you create in your life! The Workbook will help you discover astounding truths about yourself. Please continue to use it throughout the entire Course.

I recommend you read the Appendix *first*. Then, continue to refer to it as you go through the entire book. You should also begin using the relaxation technique you'll find there as soon as possible. After that, read the entire book, then go back and begin working through all the exercises and directions.

Implement the ideas and prepare to re-create yourself. I hope you'll enjoy it - have fun with it - and let me hear about the great results you're bound to achieve.

Part One

Successful Creation

Life transformation doesn't mean nothing in your life will ever change again. It means you will be at a point where you choose what will - and won't - manifest in your life. And, you will do this with full consciousness. You may embrace change anytime you wish. If your choice is for things to only get better - that's exactly what will happen.

You may be thinking that positioning yourself for creating a successful life transformation is a heck of a lot of work. I wish I could tell you otherwise. It is a lot of work and you won't do it overnight. It's true old habits die hard. Once you're on the right track, you must still be ever vigilant. It is *soooooo* easy to be sucked back into old ways of thinking and old ways of responding. You would need to become a hermit to avoid the daily influx of negative messages, and their possible influence.

The good news is that, once you can accept the principles involved, everything makes much more sense. It does get easier as you view your world in a new light. And, speaking of light - you'll actually begin to *feel* lighter pretty quickly. Yep - like the weight of the world has been lifted. That's the weight of a world that was created *for* you. The one you'll be creating for yourself is much easier to live with. You don't have to carry it. It carries you.

The first thing that will guarantee your success is the primary thing that is required for all successful creation. Commitment. You must make a *total commitment* to your own transformation. Until you do that, it's just too easy to turn back - or give up. You are completely ineffective without commitment.

Yet, that isn't even the most important reason for commitment. Commitment plays a major role in moving the universe. Once you commit to any plan - the universe moves to accomplish your plan. More help will come into your life than you could ever have imagined. Everything from being given exactly the information you need at exactly the right time - to monetary assistance - to situations opening up - to the appearance of those who can help you.

It never fails. After all, you've been committed to your old belief systems and the universe has provided exactly what you expected. Everything works both ways. Make another choice and the end result will fall in line with the new choice.

You must state your new intention. State it clearly and strongly. You may think you never stated any intention to have whatever it is in your life you'd like to eliminate. But, you did. Every time you've ever spoken of it - or thought about it - you were stating an intention. Even our acceptance of a situation states our intention that it should continue.

Whatever we give attention to - increases! It does take some time to learn the habit of controlling our thoughts and our speech. Control your thoughts - and you will control which feeling energies go out to do your creating.

This is probably a good place to mention the control of feelings. I would *never* advise you to deny your feelings. Don't be afraid of your feelings. Sure, they create - but when you take conscious control of your own creative process, *you* decide which feelings will work for you.

Feelings are simply energy. Negative fear feelings are a type of that energy. The energy of fear doesn't become problematic until it is trapped in the unconscious mind. *Always* recognize your negative feelings. Notice what you're feeling and identify the fear. Do not embrace it and claim it as yours. Simply acknowledge that it is present - make whatever perceptional changes you need to make - then allow it to pass on through.

CREATIVE TECHNIQUES

MANY different techniques will work for bringing change into your life. Creative visualization - affirmations - meditation - positive mental attitude - motivational processes - the list goes on and on. You may use one of the techniques - or a combination of all of them.

It truly doesn't matter what processes you use. Eventually, you will stop using processes altogether. That will be the day when you fully realize your Oneness with the absolute good of universal spirit. From that day forward, you will simply state your intention, expect to receive what you desire - and watch it manifest.

Until that day comes, however, you'll need some practice. Using creative techniques will allow you to begin your own creative process toward transformation. As you begin to see some success, it will reinforce for you that the principles are at work. Pay attention. One of the most prevalent reasons for failure to create the desired situations - or the loss of them later - is lack of understanding of the principles of the nature of spirit. But, most of all, those failures are caused by the failure to grasp the Principle of Oneness - with *all* life.

Sometimes we know we're ready for change - we're committed to change - but we don't have a clue which direction we should take. This can happen in any area we wish to transform. When in doubt - do nothing. If you don't know where you're going - stay where you are. Acknowledge you are ready to accept answers - then wait for them to come. They will.

Remember that you have *limitless* possibilities. Those very possibilities make responsibility - and accountability - vastly important. When you make the choice to take control of your life, you must be responsible - because you will be accountable. The universe will see to it.

Use whatever techniques are comfortable for you - and work for you. Some techniques even work that are considered a bit "off-the-wall" by the general population. The main consideration is to be sure you're not giving your own power away to a technique - or another person. It's good to have an open mind - but not so open that your brains fall out.

Some type of visualization is almost mandatory. Even inadvertently, we "see" situations in our minds before they are created. Whatever you want in life must first be envisioned. Then, you must give energy to that vision. You energize the vision with the feeling of intense desire - along with the happiness you'll feel when the desired situation manifests. Create the feeling and you'll create the manifestation of the desire.

Everything works both ways. In *"RESURRECTION,"* Neville Goddard discussed what he termed, "The Law of Reversibility." This concept explains: if a condition can bring about a certain emotional response - then the emotional response can bring about the condition. Feel and experience the joy of receiving the situation you intend to create - even before it manifests. The feeling will help create it.

If you are now manifesting something you do *not* want in your life, you must withdraw all energy from that situation. Redirect the energy toward something you *do* want. Placing blame - whining - wondering, "Why" - only gives more energy to what you don't want. Let it go. Use the energy for good and the unwanted situation will leave of its own accord in due time.

> *Fear is the ultimate negative energy. It repels your good. Love is the ultimate positive energy. It attracts the good stuff. All negative energies have their basis in fear of some type. All positive energies have their basis in love at some level. When I use the words*

"love energies," I'm referring to anything that makes you, or others, happy or creates joy.

Gratitude is another necessity for creating good. Gratitude is a form of love energy. It's hard sometimes to feel gratitude - much less express it - when life seems like a perpetual trial. Again, a change of perception is in order. Most of us wouldn't have to go far to find someone in much worse shape than we are. If you have a hard time accepting that, go out and volunteer - helping those who are in an exaggerated condition to yours.

In addition to raising your level of gratitude, you'll also be giving what you wish to receive. If you need assistance - give assistance. If you need love - give love. If you need money - give money. Using the Principle of Oneness, whatever you give to others, you are giving to yourself. Everything you freely give will come back to you, multiplied many times over. It probably won't come back to you from the same source where you gave - but it will come back. Often, in most surprising ways - and sometimes, just when you need it most.

Deprivation-Consciousness

Anytime we want something we apparently don't have, we assume a consciousness of lack - or deprivation. This can be one of the most difficult fear feelings to overcome. When we take on a fear-consciousness from something we don't have, everything we feel, think or do comes from that place of fear.

If money is short, every financial decision is based on fear the money won't be there. If we don't have satisfying relationships, we decide what we can - or cannot - do, based on the fear of doing it alone. If we don't see ourselves as youthful and vigorous, we spend inordinate amounts of time worrying about our health and aging process. When we are expressing deprivation-consciousness, we're constantly making our life decisions around the fear of what will happen due to our perceived lack.

Obviously, this only makes matters worse. We're giving almost constant attention to a condition we don't want. Steadily supplying it with energy to create more of the same situation. A lot of it is completely automatic and we don't realize we're doing it. I get a lot of resistance from clients who have allowed themselves to be sucked into this type of consciousness. I hear, "I can't help it if I feel poor - or lonely - or old."

Yes, we can help it. We can change those feelings with our thoughts. We had to look around in the first place and mentally make a decision those conditions exist. Then, the feelings took over. We can just as easily re-think the situation and make different choices. In other words, we change our mind-set to something more positive. And, I might add, more true.

Following are some of the positive mind-sets that will help you to achieve the positive view you need to have to proceed with this Course:

Positive Mind-Sets ...

- The universe is infinitely good and has already provided everything I need or want. If I don't see it, either I haven't called it into manifestation - or it hasn't reached me yet.

- I'm totally committed to achieving my desire and I take whatever steps I can *right now* to bring it about.

- I'm ready and willing to receive *now* and I expect my intended outcome.

- I do whatever I can each day to feel rich - give love - be kind to myself.

- Every cell in my body has inherent intelligence and I direct my cells' activity; sending them love and positive instructions.

- Whatever conditions I'm experiencing right now are *temporary* and I'm happy and excited my desires are being accomplished.

Take Action:

Go over these mind-sets until you begin to feel the truth in them. Learn them thoroughly and associate them with what is going on during the course of your day.

It is vitally important you bring your belief system into accord with these mind-sets. As you are learning – begin to act on the statements consciously as often as you can.

Although it certainly can't hurt, these statements don't have to be made as affirmations. It's much more important to consistently create the *feelings* surrounding the truth of the statements. Envision what life will be like when your desires manifest. Smile when you think about it! Go through your day with an attitude of happy expectancy. Then, the universe knows exactly what you expect.

It's also important to eliminate anger and frustration as much as possible. These are fear-based feelings. They'll eventually dissolve as you begin to replace fear with love.

Signs of Land

I'll share with you a neat little trick for sustaining that feeling of happy expectancy. Look for "signs of land." Sometimes we turn away our greater good because we don't recognize or accept the first evidence that it's on its way. One more time - *pay attention!*

If you're creating financial prosperity, finding a designer dress for $25 in a resale shop is a sign of land. The nickel laying on the sidewalk is a sign of land. Your boss gives you tickets to an event - sign of land.

You're creating a new relationship. A friend sets you up on a blind date. It isn't a person you'd like to start a relationship with, but it is a sign of land. You receive an ad in the mail for a singles activity - sign of land. Even your first time notice of a billboard showing a happy couple, engaged in one of your favorite activities, can be a sign of land. Project yourself right into that picture.

You are creating health, or physical well-being. You catch a cold but it only lasts two days instead of the usual week - sign of land. You wake up one morning and your fingers aren't stiff - sign of land. You put on a favorite outfit and the waistband is more comfortable than usual - sign of land.

Signs of land *always* show up and usually begin with very small things related to your desire coming into your life. They need to recognized - and appreciated - in order to expand the energies. Always give deep and sincere thanks for every small sign. Finding a dollar bill in the pocket of an old jacket, then complaining because it isn't a 20 dollar bill, is counterproductive.

"Signs of land" are signals your intended creation is on the way. You can stop the flow on the spot with refusal to recognize and accept small gifts. Watching for - accepting - and giving thanks - for these small signals will help sustain your positive feelings - which can only hasten your manifestation.

Take Action:

Begin watching for "signs of land" on a daily basis. Do not decide ahead of time what they need to be. Start learning now to get in the habit of watching for these signs.

Write down your desires. As you recognize each sign that a desire is on its way to you - write that down too. Don't do it dispassionately. Involve your feelings! Feel the gratitude that your desire is manifesting as deeply as possible. Give thanks!

During the course of your life transformation, you will experience times when everything appears to come to a screeching halt. Don't panic. That will only regenerate old fears. This is a perfectly appropriate situation. During those "down-times," your consciousness is assimilating your new outlooks and beliefs.

When you begin to move forward again, you'll find you have made *major* advances. Suddenly, things will begin moving at an accelerated pace as your new - stabilized - consciousness kicks in.

To prepare yourself for those downtimes, condition yourself through reward, right from the beginning. Reward yourself for each, and every, small success until your complete transformation takes place. You are bound to experience those times when everything seems to be "on hold." That is the natural order of things. Self-rewards will help you move through those times without giving in to the urge to give up.

Your Health - Your Wealth
Your Happiness

In the next chapters I'll give you some specific mind-sets for each of the three main areas of life - prosperity - health - and relationships. I'll relate those processes to specific principles so you may generalize them for your own specific purposes.

In *The MASTER COURSE* - Part Two through Part Four - I give very specific techniques in specific areas of creation.

Principles of Transformation

What is meant by "principle?" Let's define our terms. A principle is an unchanging, fundamental basis of nature - or the universe. Think about the principles of mathematics. 2 + 2 = 4. *Every time!* No matter what you do, 2 + 2 can never equal five. Even if a child believes with all his heart that 2 + 2 equals five, that doesn't make it so. It is *unchangeable*.

We don't *do* mathematics. We use the principles of math to arrive at certain conclusions. The science of physics shows everything in our universe can be reduced to a mathematical equation. The principles always work by themselves - and they *always* give us the same exact conclusions. Provided we understand the principles.

Now, don't confuse "fact" with "principle." A fact is changeable. "Facts" often change as more knowledge is gained. 200 years ago, it was a fact that no machine could fly. Yet today, we circle our planet routinely - in the machine called the airplane. It's also a fact that, aerodynamically, the bumblebee can't fly. And yet, unaware of our scientific "facts," he continues to buzz around the garden completely unconcerned that he isn't designed for flight. So much for facts!

Also, please don't confuse "law" with "principle." A universal principle is the *underlying basis* of a universal law. For instance, the law of cause and effect is the result of the principle, which states, "Spirit is the Moving Force." Remember, *principle never changes*. Change a cause and you'll change the effect - but the underlying principle works exactly the same. The law is the action of the principle. (The specific universal laws will be discussed at the beginning of Part Three.)

Over 1500 years ago, the great philosopher, St. Augustine, said, *"Miracles are not contrary to nature, but only contrary to what we know about nature."* It's pretty sad we believe it takes a "miracle" to accomplish what is actually the natural order of things.

Yet, that in itself is proof of how powerful we truly are. We can take the natural order of things and muck it up until when - we finally give up trying to make 2 + 2 = 5 - we ask for a miracle - and get out of the way - the natural order of things produces our "miracle."

These principles are often thought of as metaphysical. The word "metaphysical" means 'beyond the physical' - which is then described as the "spiritual."

It's more accurate to define the principles involved as *"super-physical."* It is now known that what was once thought of as purely spiritual is demonstrated in physicality. All that was beyond us was the knowledge of these scientific facts.

It has been proven within the scientific community that everything in our universe is created from energy. This knowledge has come from the study of quantum physics - the study of sub-atomic particles within the atom. Every material object we have is constructed from matter. All matter can be reduced to atoms.

As scientists have reduced the atom to its smallest components, they finally arrived at the center. What they found was what we might call "nothing." The smallest component of the atoms, which make up everything we "see" on the planet, appears in the form of energy packets - or *light!* Energy.

This means your computer, your car, your clothing, even your body itself, is basically nothing more than light. Not that light is anything to be discounted. What is light? It's energy - the life force of the universe. And, energy works through the use of principles - just like math.

Even thoughts and feelings have a measurable energy and affect our physical bodies in various ways depending upon the aspects of that energy. Some type of energy is used to create every single part of our lives. I constantly hear people say, "Everything happens for a reason." That's 100% true. But, I always wonder if they realize the reason is because we are master manipulators of energy.

We can - and do - create everything in our lives through our manipulation of energy. In some cases, we accept certain situations into our lives because, at some level, we have agreed to the learning contained within them. We do it whether we are consciously aware of it or not. Some we do consciously - some we do unconsciously - and some we do at the deepest level of our spirit. Our spirit being that part of us we know exists - and serves some higher purpose.

We have three levels of mind: the conscious - or thinking - mind, the unconscious - or feeling - mind, and the superconscious - or knowing - mind. Our spirit lies within our superconscious mind.

Our challenge is to able to move energy in such a way as to create *only* what we want in our lives - and continue to do it in such a way it becomes transformation. Now, how can we do that if part of what we create comes from our unconscious (feeling) or superconscious (spirit) minds and we're unaware of it?

First, we must learn and accept the basic principles of creation. That, in turn, will open our perceptions so we can know what lies within the unconscious and within our personal spirit. Then, everything becomes conscious. We are no longer trying to create something consciously while our unconscious is hollering, "NO!"

I tend to disagree with those who believe we need to fear what is in our unconscious minds. The unconscious is merely the filing cabinet where we stuff things we don't want - or don't need - to think about. This includes habits as well as pain and fear.

Later, I'll explain why it's so important that we understand what we fear. We can't understand what we don't remember. And, it's easy to bring those things to the surface in a completely safe manner when we accept the basic principles of our universe.

Universal Principles

Universal principles are the principles of the nature of our universal spirit. These are the inherent qualities of the creation. To think of the universe as simply a physical system of planetary and cosmic bodies is a mistake.

In order to effect a positive life transformation, we need to understand we are connected, via energy (light), to everything in creation - all energy in creation helps us to support life - and spirit itself is that energy.

When I use the term, "universal spirit," I'm simply referring to the universal life force. This life force is the energy we use to create everything in our lives. We are surrounded by this energy at all times. We live within the energy - just as the energy lives within us. We are co-creators with this universal spirit.

Nearly everyone will admit something drives the universe. Those who believe life is merely a series of nonsensical random accidents haven't been paying attention. There is order in the universe.

We must understand the principles of the nature of the universal spirit. Our individual spirit is our greatest source of energy since it is a part, or aspect, of the universal spirit. The word "spirit" itself is defined as "breath." The breath of life - or - the energy of life.

When we accept these principles of spirit, we lose all fear. *Fear* is the reason people who begin to create happier lives for themselves eventually begin to backslide. The most powerful thing you can learn is to overcome fear. Fear is an aspect of death energy.

Now, I didn't say to deny fear. Fear itself is just an energy, which we ourselves create. When we can accept the principles of the nature of *spirit*, we stop creating fear. Then, and only then, are we headed toward a complete life transformation.

Let's take a look at the principles. Remember - you must be willing to bring yourself to accept the truth of these universal principles before you can hope to transform your life. Changing your perspective is the most important thing you can do toward life transformation. In fact, it's mandatory.

Since all principles of spirit are inherently positive, you may wonder how you can ever create anything "negative." This is simply because no judgment exists in the universal spirit. We can create whatever we like. The labels of "good" or "bad" are our own.

Life is an eternal energy. Eternal. Now, rather than go into all the esoteric explanations concerning whether death exists (which is an oxymoron in itself), let's approach this from another angle entirely.

Let's assume someone - or something - goes into that state we call "death." From a strictly physical standpoint, that material body is going to undergo some changes. Even the cells of a body are made up of substance. Given a long enough period of time (time is meaningless in terms of eternity anyway) - and provided they aren't preserved in some way - those physical cells will eventually completely disappear from all physicality.

Ultimately, the cells will return to their original existence as substance, or light - and hence, energy. On this basis alone, all the arguments concerning whether there is such a condition as "death" are irrelevant. Life is an eternal activity of energy.

As you read through these principles, remember:

- The most powerfully creative part of you is your individual spirit - that part which recognizes you serve some higher purpose.

- We are speaking of the principles of the *nature* of spirit.

- Your individual spirit *can never be separated* from the universal spirit.

- Your individual spirit already *knows* these principles. Our purpose here is to help you remember by bringing them to your conscious mind for acceptance.

Spirit is Power

All power comes directly from spirit - our personal power, as well as universal power. It's all part of the same power that is the energy of creative life force.

Since we're always connected with spirit, there can never be a time that we're powerless. Never! Whether or not we choose to use our power for positive purposes is another story altogether. The choice is 100% ours. Anytime we choose to tap into it, we have unlimited power to accomplish whatever we choose to create.

It's unfortunate we tend to think of our personal power as something based in ego. Or, something that is somehow associated with our personalities - or even our capabilities. Those perceptions are completely erroneous. In fact, there is not a single person on this planet who is more powerful than anyone else. We *all* have access to - and ability to use - the absolute power of spirit at any time we choose.

Spirit is Creator

As the basis of creation, spirit is our source of everything. The very definition of "superconscious" tells us we *do* have a consciousness that is *fully aware* of our absolute and unchanging connection to spirit.

Since we do have super-consciousness, at some level we *know* we are co-creators with a universal spirit. At that level, we *know* exactly who we are. At that level, we *know* we carry all of the aspects of the universal spirit. At that level, no fear can be present.

Spirit is Absolute Good

This is the most basic principle. We never create anything we would consider "negative" for ourselves without first creating the fear energy. Fear is a purely human emotion. Our personal internal spirit - or superconscious mind - knows nothing about fear.

Fear has been labeled as "bad." Let's take a look at that. There was a time when fear was necessary to our very survival. It's an emotion we developed to literally stay alive in order to propagate our species. Its basic use was for our physical survival.

Even today, it has its uses. Fear is the emotion that would come up if you were standing in a convenience store at 3 AM and someone walked in waving a gun. It might cause you to slam on the brakes when the car in front of you starts to swerve out of control. Fear is an automatic response to insure our physical safety. It always has been. But, I like to call that response "caution."

The fear that keeps us from creating the lives we want is fear for our emotional well-being. It is ego-based and very much concerned with avoiding emotional pain. This is the fear we can - and must - eradicate through knowledge of this universal principle - *spirit is absolute good*. When we accept the truth of this principle, we know everything works for good. I understand it's hard to see sometimes. Yet, if we take the time to look, we'll find the positive purpose in every situation.

Spirit is Substance

Substance is the energy that lies under all manifestation. It is the basis of matter. Again, that substance is energy - or light. It's there to be used for creation of all tangible objects. Since spirit is substance, it isn't difficult to see that spirit exists even in physical objects. Our very bodies are built from substance. Substance is the foundation of everything we create in our material world. All matter comes from spirit.

Spirit is the Moving Force

Spirit is the catalyst, which moves our world forward. In order to create, energies must move out into the universe, finding like energies to form the desired creation.

Remember: spirit is energy and energy is light. Light can never stand still. In fact, by its very nature, no energy can be static - or it ceases to be energy. All energy we embrace within ourselves as "ours," will radiate out to go about its job of creation in the universe. Whether we are aware of this movement or not has no bearing on the situation. It's a fundamental principle of spirit and operates with - or without - our knowledge or consent.

Spirit is Mind

Here we're talking about *universal mind*. This is the origin and the source of all knowledge. I'm sure you've heard the expression, "There's nothing new under the sun." This is an absolute truth. Everything that has ever been - or will ever be - created, has been in existence since the beginning of creation. The substance for everything already exists in the universal mind just waiting to be brought into manifestation.

Each of the ideas most important to the evolution of our advancement throughout history, were "invented" at about the same time - in several different places. Archeological evidence shows several different civilizations began using fire at about the same time. The same thing happened with the use of the wheel. Did this knowledge physically transfer from one civilization to another? No. These ancient societies of people were separated by vast distances and had no way of communicating from group to group at that point in history.

We are all connected to each other through this universal mind. It's been proven scientifically when one atom moves, it can affect other atoms even on the other side of the world. The ideas were brought forth into manifestation by one civilization, then instantly became available through universal mind to all others.

Spirit is Law

Law is the action of principle. Technically, 2 + 2 = 4 is the law based on the principle that when 2 objects are added (action) to 2 more objects - there will be a total of 4 objects. So, a law is the outcome of a principle in operation. This is a good concept to learn well. Then, you'll always be able to reduce any universal law to its underlying principle, thereby affecting the outcome in your favor.

The principles of the nature of spirit are always in operation. As the moving force of the universe, spirit is dynamic - always in action.

Spirit is Love

Love is the harmonizing principle of the universe. It is *always* present because spirit is always present. In our world of polarity, love is the opposite of fear. Fear certainly brings discordant situations into our lives. Love, on the other hand, brings the situations which allow us to live in peace and harmony.

Too much of the time, we're on autopilot - the unconscious mind is in control. When we're operating from our unconscious minds, we create many things through the use of the energies (feelings) of fear. When we operate from our superconscious (which is pretty rare) we can never bring anything but harmonious situations into our lives.

What we can easily do, however, is learn and accept the principles of the nature of spirit. Then we can operate more directly from our conscious minds until the new habits become unconscious and replace the fear energies.

Within our spirit, love is always *unconditional*. There is no judgment - so no conditions can be present.

Spirit is Grace

Grace is the rounding out of all principles. What many refer to as "karma," is actually a Universal Law, which says, "What goes out must come back." There's an interesting attribute to this particular law, which I believe is grace.

This Universal Law comes up when people think about being "paid back" for what they do. It seems if we do something - either loving or unloving - we should receive back exactly in the same proportion we gave. Not true. Since the nature of spirit is absolute good - not to mention, love - grace seems to kick in with this law.

Do something loving and we will receive the good back multiplied. Do something unloving (which will only be done out of fear) and we never seem to receive back as much as we gave. *Grace!* An absolute principle of the nature of spirit.

Principle of Oneness

I'VE been telling you about the principles of the *nature of spirit*. Now, having said all that, I may have a surprise for you. *Only ONE principle exists in the universe.* I've been mentioning that principle all the way through the definitions of the nature of spirit. Did you catch it?

The *One Principle* is the *Principle of Oneness*! All other universal principles I prefer to think of as "sub-principles." Sub-principles exist only because of the Principle of Oneness. The One Principle states there can be no separation in any part of spirit. *Everything* is connected and part of *spirit*. The universal spirit is *you* on an expanded scale.

The most, minute components of energy are inter-related. Nothing stands alone. It isn't possible to have an effect on an individual atom without affecting other atoms. Every action affects the whole.

All attributes, which apply to the universal spirit, also apply to your personal spirit - existing as your superconscious mind. It's *exactly* the same. The only reason we don't express those attributes in our daily lives is that we live from the ego of our conscious - and the feelings of our unconscious - minds.

As co-creators with universal energy - or spirit - our intent is to live life in the physical with the "appearance" of separation - until we remember who we are. Then, we will live only from our superconscious minds. To be more accurate - the illusions of the conscious and unconscious will dissolve and meld into our one true mind. The superconscious.

Let's examine this concept of Oneness. It's absolutely necessary to understand this if you wish to live the life of your dreams. Every technique you use - every process - depends upon your understanding of Oneness. Otherwise, you will experience the discouraging situations of either failure in your creative efforts - or - whatever you create will fade away with time.

Now, let's go back to that convenience store mentioned earlier: the one where a person comes in waving a gun. I've already explained how we are all interconnected. This means we are One with the gun waver. In fact, we're even One with the gun! There can be no separation of energies.

At some level we have agreed to be a part of this scenario - for our own learning. Or, we wouldn't be there at that moment in time. When we look at the person with the gun, we are seeing an aspect of ourselves. It's usually an aspect we have denied - "I could never do that," - and need to accept. Everything in front of us is a mirror to ourselves. Put there so we can see ourselves - and accept every part of ourselves with love. No judgments need to be involved here. Believe it or not - everyone is capable of doing all things - under certain, very specific, circumstances for each of us. We don't need to judge ourselves for that - we only need to accept it. Everyone - at some point in their life - does something they swore they'd never do based upon one judgment or another.

We'll come out much better if we direct love toward every person in front of us, with the understanding we are looking at an aspect of ourselves. If we allow fear to go out instead, it's likely to create quite another situation.

Of course, I just gave you a pretty scary scenario. But, the situation is the same regardless of who - or what - is in front of you. If, before her passing, you had been walking down the street in New York while Mother Teresa was visiting, and recognized her on the street - the same principles would apply. You would be looking at an aspect of yourself. You would be at that particular place - at that particular time - so you could see another part of yourself, which for some reason you needed to see.

How to Use This Information

The absolute principle that connects all life needs to be integrated into consciousness. In our humanity, we split ourselves into ethnic or political groups, religions, countries, etc. Then, more often than not, we begin to kill each other off due to philosophical differences. We *always* pay the price for that!

We are ONE with everyone else! No matter what labels we place on ourselves - we can never change that. 2 + 2 will *always* equal 4. When living a life where we consciously take total creative power, we need to remember that every minute. The Principle of Oneness underlies some basic universal *laws*.

For instance, "What goes out must come back." And, the Law of Reversibility - "Everything works both ways." Because of the Principle of Oneness, what we do to another - we do to ourselves. What we wish for another - we wish for ourselves. When we take life - we lose life.

We must watch our words, our thoughts and our judgments. Our thoughts and words have no power to create - but our feelings do. Feelings are the energy behind our thoughts. Words are the vehicle for those feelings. So, remove the negative judgments, and you'll change the fear feelings behind those judgments to the energy of love.

All of this is a matter of changing our perceptions about what's going on in any given moment. Generalize it to any situation. Accepting our Oneness - acting from our Oneness - opens our superconscious minds. When we're living from the superconscious mind, there's no way the universe can send us anything but absolute good. There's no way we can fail to create exactly what it is we desire.

Love is the most powerful creative energy in the universe!

Replacing Attitudes & Beliefs

It's our attitudes and beliefs (including judgments) that so often throw us curves when we're trying to use the creative processes consciously. None of us have congenital belief systems. We were not born with them. Everything we believe has come from some kind of experience. We have several options for making the needed changes.

Some beliefs actually have very little feeling behind them. Yet, our acceptance of them specifies our intent that the universe should support them. And, the universe does. These beliefs are usually based on "facts" reported to us by someone we perceived to be an authority. This particular type of belief is fairly easy to discard with some concentrated effort. All it takes is a bit of rational thought and an intent to release it from our definition of who we are. But, it can be done.

First, of course, you have to be aware you hold a particular belief. All that's really required here is to pay attention. My two favorite words: "Pay attention!" You'll be as amazed as I was when I first started "hearing" my own thoughts and words. Maybe "appalled" would be a better word.

For a while you'll need to question nearly every statement you hear yourself thinking or saying. Beliefs are always stated as fact. Remember, that when you make a statement of fact, you are sending energies out into the universe to bring back situations to support your statement. Just because you've seen evidence that a belief is true doesn't necessarily make it so. You may have simply created that truth for yourself.

When you question your belief systems, you'll need to be very honest with yourself. Is it true because you want it to be true? Does it serve you in a positive way? Who told you it was true in the first place? Is that person's truth something you want to be true for you? Does it serve a higher purpose for your life?

In other words, is it based in love - or fear? Any belief based in fear will ultimately be a detriment to positive life transformation.

When you find the nonsensical beliefs (and you will), it merely takes a bit rational thought to put them right. It could be as simple as, "Girls can't do math." - "Men are insensitive," - or even, "People put on weight when they reach middle-age." When you accept the judgments of others for yourself, you are giving away your power. It can never be taken from you - it can only be given away.

Many of our beliefs come from outside authorities. "Ragweed makes you sneeze." Well, it sure does if you believe it does. Nothing is more powerful than you. You decide how the cells of your body are going to respond to everything from ragweed to aging.

I'll admit some beliefs are so firmly implanted - and have so much apparent evidence behind them - it seems impossible at first to overcome them. You must change some of these beliefs by using constant reference to the principle of absolute good. What the rest of the world is expressing has absolutely nothing to do with what you choose to express personally. And, by "express," I mean manifest.

Other beliefs have been implanted with lots of fear feelings surrounding them. Many of these are messages that have been communicated to you over the years. Usually they relate to what's possible for you personally. Most of these messages have taken up residence in your unconscious mind and the feelings surrounding them constantly create situations to prove their validity.

The unconscious mind is very powerful because it isn't attached - or holding on - to these feelings. Those are the only feelings it knows with regard to a particular belief and those feelings are free to go right on out and create their evidence.

In "Life and Teaching of the Masters of the Far East," Baird T. Spalding wrote:

> *"We, ourselves, delegate mastery to people or situations. Once we give that mastery, we accept - and experience - the feelings we recognize as existing in the nature of that mastery. We obey the master we have assigned by embracing the feelings we believe it has the power to create in us. Then the moment we say, "I am (that)" - we become one with it."*

For instance, you may give another person the right to make you angry. Once you have given that right, you accept the feelings you recognize in that master. Then, you obey the master - that you proclaimed - by experiencing the expected feelings. The moment you say something like - "I'm mad every time I see that guy," - you instantly *become* that anger. You, alone, create the anger with your use of the words, "I AM ..."

Before emotional beliefs can be corrected, we have to remember what they are - and how they moved in originally. We also have to identify the feelings involved with each belief. Following each remembrance and identification, you'll need to decide how the feelings implanted with each memory can be changed. You can go through years of therapy for this.

As an alternative, you can use my Guide to Personal Self-Analysis, *"Who's Driving Your Bus?"* This guide serves as the Workbook for *The MASTER COURSE* and contains the same questions I've used so successfully with my own clients in spiritual therapy sessions. It also provides appropriate techniques for changing your personal fear feelings into positive feelings for life transformation. The Workbook is the Appendix of this book.

Beliefs and attitudes that restrict our ability to create the desires of our hearts may be termed "dysfunctional." Any belief and/or attitude which is in line with the primary principle of the universe - the Principle of Oneness - will *always* create in a positive manner. These beliefs are driven only by feelings of love. Upon reflection, you'll see any positive emotion comes from love.

Often, you'll find there doesn't seem to be any way to change a core belief feeling. The hurt behind the fear is far too strong. This is when we use the most powerful of transformative tools … a change of perception.

Change of Perception

Can you remember a time when someone hurt your feelings badly - without meaning to? Maybe a friend made a comment you perceived as critical. You probably experienced hurt - and fear that in some way you didn't measure up. Later, you found out your friend had no intention of being critical, and you had perceived the comment in an entirely different light than it was offered.

Two things would have shifted when you discovered the true intent behind the comment. First, your perception of the comment itself would shift. No harm was intended. No defensive fear response is necessary. Secondly, you would "get over" any animosity you felt toward the friend for being critical. This is a type of forgiveness, albeit, there is nothing to forgive. Most importantly, you would move on without any new feelings of fear about yourself.

When reviewing old memories to see where we acquired fear feelings, the others involved in those memories aren't always available to us for consultation. Even if they are available, they may be unable to understand our feelings.

If that's the case, you have the challenge of changing your perception regarding a situation - exactly the way it seemed to you at the time. Not always an easy task. You will find the techniques for accomplishing this process in *The MASTER COURSE* Workbook, "Who's Driving Your Bus?"

Do know this. If you can't see a rational reason why your more disharmonious beliefs are incorrect - you must change your perception of the memories behind the beliefs. If you don't, the fear feelings behind those disharmonious belief systems will continue to create disharmonious situations in your life.

Love is the *most* powerful force in the universe. Love will *always* heal and transform fear.

Prosperity and Wealth

This chapter is dedicated to helping you increase your financial wealth. This is a major concern for almost everyone. There never seems to be enough. And, that is a mind-set that needs to be adjusted immediately. Before we get into actual financial wealth, I need to see if I can help you with that adjustment.

When "prosperity" is defined only as "financial wealth," the definition is much too narrow. Prosperity covers much more than money. When we begin to look at prosperity from this position, it's fairly easy to get over that "not enough" syndrome. In leading a prosperous life we need to create prosperity in *all* areas.

You can be rich in your relationships. Don't tell me nobody loves you. Look around and examine all of your relationships. Family of origin - children - friends - neighbors - intimate relationships - even associates at work. Sure, most of us have relationships that could be improved. But, for the most part, people who are in our lives for any period of time, are continually gifting us with love - in one form or another.

Any gift we receive from another person is a form of love energy. It can be a spoken compliment - time spent helping out - the loan of a rake - a hug - a referral from a business associate. These gifts come much more often than we think about. They're from the neighbor who buys that Little League raffle ticket from your kid - the sister who gives you the sweater she bought that didn't fit her after all or, the brother who helps you move. They're from the friend who tells you your "do" isn't working - the boss who says, "Good job!" - The spouse who calls when she is going to be late.

You can be rich in your physical well-being. You breeze through what is purported to be "allergy season" - you can still fit into your wedding dress/military uniform - you rarely catch a cold - you can walk to the mailbox without panting for breath - you have more hair than your best friend from high school.

You may be rich in talent - rich in your children - rich in humor. Do you see where I'm going with this? Anything we have a lot of - makes us rich. We all have an abundance of those things if we just know where to look. So, before you go about creating financial prosperity, take a look around. Make a list of everything you *already have* in abundance. If you can't see it - pay attention.

Start watching and noting everything you receive in a day - whether physical or emotional - no matter how small. Then, begin expressing gratitude for each one of those things - as they happen. You are now directing energy into the universe to bring you more of the "good stuff." Remember, complaining about what we don't have only gives the "lack" situation more energy.

Your next assignment is to realize - and accept that *you are always rich!* At the superconscious level, we're always aware there can be no lack - of any kind. At the very deepest levels of your being, you already know this. We are each eternally connected to all the energies that create anything we desire.

Through this connection, we have constant access to those energies. Each of us has equal access to the very same energies that bring fortunes into the lives of the wealthiest people on Earth.

The Principle of Oneness demands that, if one has wealth - we all have it. Whether or not we choose to express wealth in our lives, is completely up to us. Can't make the car payment? Make another decision. Notice I don't bother to say, "Make another choice." We can choose all day long, every day. But, until we made a *decision*, nothing changes.

Decisions imply intent. The moment you express your intent to make a change, you also make a commitment. Provided your intent is clear.

We can't always be certain we have clear intent. The only way to find out is to ask yourself. Think, for a moment, about something you want. Let's assume your wish is for financial wealth. Now think about all the people you've heard of who were wealthy beyond measure. Were they happy? Maybe - maybe not. If not, why not?

Contrary to popular opinion, money can buy a heck of a lot of happiness. But, it can also bring heartache and misery. This isn't a news flash to anyone. Since we all have some knowledge of this, we also have some unconscious fear feelings about it. These are the "Yes, buts" that our unconscious sends out to garble our intent.

"Yes, but what if I get a lot of money and - people take advantage of me - I can't manage it - the IRS takes half of it (they will) - I just create bigger debts - my friends get jealous?"

You need to handle this right up front when you begin to create financial prosperity. Sit down and ask yourself if there are possible situations surrounding having wealth that you don't want in your life. You may be surprised at what comes up for you. Are you capable and willing to handle all the details of administering a vast estate?

"I'll hire someone to do it for me." Okay. Are you sure? Do you have any fears surrounding that?

Before I cause you to sigh in resignation, I'll remind you of one of the principles of the nature of life: Life is Absolute Good! When you can realize this - and accept it - all fear of the unknown leaves. You create a new core belief, based in love feelings, which assures you will not create additional problems around having your wishes granted.

Take Action:

Your first step toward positioning yourself for financial wealth is to work through the things I mentioned above. Take some time to think about them deeply – in relation to your own life situation. Write down all the feelings that come up for you as you consider how you would actually handle great wealth.

Let It Go

Quite a number of years ago, I knew I needed to change career direction. I was bored with my business and growing quite restless. I felt very pressed, from within, to make that change. I thought about it for several weeks, trying to decide what to do. I had been self-employed for many years and my skills were highly specialized - they wouldn't generalize well to the job market.

Finally, I became so frustrated, I was about to give up ever having a single good idea. One evening, I threw up my hands and practically hollered at the universe. I told the universe I knew I was supposed to make a change - I was sick of trying to figure it out - and the universe could just do it for me.

I said I would look at the employment ads every day to try to get some ideas - and I would start talking to people about it. And, I adamantly stated this was all I was going to do - I would not spend any further effort trying to come up with ideas. End of discussion.

What I accomplished with my little fit at the universe was this. I effectively released all the energy I had been holding inside me while I wrestled with my decision regarding a new career path. I had been so intent on doing it for myself I'd forgotten the universe will always help - if allowed to. Yet, the universe could not help as long as I held tight to my own creative energy. In my frustration, I had surrendered - and I had finally released the energy.

The very next day, not one - but two - excellent possibilities were laid right at my feet. One came from 1200 miles away. Out of the blue - no possible way to suspect they would turn up. What really blew me away was that both people who contacted me told me they had just had a sudden idea, along with the impulse to contact me about it.

As long as I'm telling this story, I might as well tell you the silly part too. You may learn something from it. Each of the ideas presented to me were perfect for my abilities, both were exciting, and both would require considerable effort on my part. One would require me to relocate 1200 miles away; the other would require me to return to college for post-graduate work.

I chose what looked like the easiest of the options - and relocated. It lasted less than six months. Then I regrouped and resumed my education. The lesson is this: What the universe provides is not always a done deal. There's always something left for us to do - even if it's to make the right choice. Of course, the primary lesson is to ask for help. When in doubt - do nothing. Ask for help - expect help - and wait until you're shown what to do.

Also, remember that every insane idea that pops into our heads isn't necessarily from our own spirit-consciousness. True, we need to be open to all universal ideas. If it's an idea for our highest good, it will always be reinforced by being shown to us in more than one way. It will also work. If you have a continuous struggle to make it work for you, you may have hooked into someone else's idea. Don't be afraid to start over.

I'd like to mention one other thing here ...

I refer to it as, "The greatest pressure always happens just before the breakthrough." Consider the astronaut who is flying into outer space. As the rocket goes up into space, the pressure on the astronaut becomes stronger and stronger - pushing him back into the seat. Finally, the pressure becomes so great he may feel as through the body is about to be crushed. When, suddenly, the rocket breaks through the gravity barrier and all pressure is released.

A similar feeling often happens when we are wrestling with a problem. Just at the moment when we feel as if the problem itself is about to crush us - we surrender. At that very moment, the pressure is released into the universe for resolution.

So, don't be afraid when the pressure seems overwhelming. That may be your signal you are about to make a breakthrough!

Take Action:

Find some small ways where you can practice letting go. Don't try the big stuff at first. You don't want to defeat yourself by setting up fear. Be very specific. Let go of as much control as you comfortably can. Practice turning the problem over to the universe. Then take whatever small steps you can take today toward your goal.

If the Desire Is Yours the Manifestation Is Yours

WHEN you're sure your intent is clear and you make your commitment, the next step is to begin using whatever creative techniques you have chosen. Then, start taking whatever steps you can take *right now toward* your goal. Even baby steps. My decision, in the example above - to look at ads and network - were "baby steps."

Once again, the Principle of Oneness necessitates that you recognize your connection to your desire. If you sit and wait for it to suddenly appear, without any involvement on your own part, you are creating separation. You must do something to make yourself one with the desired creation.

The "Act as if ..." idea comes into play here. If you want to be rich - you'll need to feel rich. Start with the ideas I mentioned earlier. Connect your feelings to all the areas of your life that are already rich in gifts for you. That in itself will go a long way toward removing poverty-consciousness.

It's also a good idea to create ways to cause yourself to feel financially rich. Now, I don't mean to write checks on money you don't have in the bank. But, it is good to change your thinking regarding money. It isn't that you don't have it - it's that it isn't in the bank *yet*. Go ahead and pick out some of the things you want to spend it on when it does appear in your account.

Intend to have them. Buy yourself something that makes you feel rich regularly. Very small things work just fine. Have the cronut, rather than the donut. Find a really good sweater at a re-sale shop rather than spending the same money for a cheap one at a discount store.

Look at your surroundings. Then, start pitching. Get rid of all the junk. Have a garage or yard sale - sell all the little knickknacks - the clothes that don't fit - the sports equipment you never use - even some of the good stuff you do have. If you're tired of it - or you don't use it - sell it! Then, buy a few good decorative items - and few good pieces of clothing – one, good tennis racket - with the proceeds.

Look at your vehicle. Are you going to treat your new Lexus like that? Okay, so it's old. Wash and wax it anyway. Clean out the Big Mac wrappers and install a litterbag. Clean up the yard (if you have one) or make a window box. Then, plant a few flowers. Start with the ones you can buy at 6 for a dollar. Then, take care of them. Encourage growth (expansion) energy by cultivating anything that grows.

When we have a poverty-consciousness, we tend to act as if nothing we have is valuable. We often neglect our homes, our vehicles, sometimes even ourselves. We act as if nothing will make any difference. It *does* make a difference.

It makes a difference in how we feel - and our feelings are what will go out into the universe and create more of what we already have. Bring even one nice object into your life - make it yours - and I'll guarantee your desire for more will create some powerful new feelings. And - your commitment level will go way up.

Everything expands. The universe itself expands. Whatever you give energy to - will expand. We have to give our energy to things in a positive way so they will expand in a positive way. Ever heard the expression, "The rich get richer, and the poor get poorer?" There's a kernel of truth there.

Where are the rich putting their energy of feeling and expectation? And where are the poor putting theirs? You can easily change your focus!

What we bless will also expand. However, this is one of those places to be careful. I once had an old car and I despised that car. But, I wanted another car, so I verbally blessed it every time I got in it - but I still despised it in my heart. Well, six months later - I had two old cars.

You see, I may have blessed my old car but I neglected to change my feelings. The blessing merely expanded my negative feelings. Had I generated some gratitude that I had a car at all, when I blessed it, things would have turned out differently.

Health, Youth & Physical Well-Being

This is often the most difficult area of life to convince students they can control through creative techniques. Thousands of so-called "miracle cures" happen every year and we hear about them frequently. In reality, our bodies are the easiest place to have absolute creative control. Your body belongs strictly to you. Contrary to popular opinion, you don't have to concern yourself about what other people choose that will have an effect on you.

Yet, nothing is more ingrained in us than the belief that we are born - we age - and we die. By the time we experience all of the expected diseases and the dreaded aging process, death begins to look pretty good.

If we could ever learn to use the universal energies in a perfect and habitual manner, we would never be ill - we would never show signs of age past maturity - and we would only "die" when we made a conscious choice to leave our physical bodies.

Needless to say, I get a lot of objections to that idea. (But then, I'm known as a divergent thinker - and I have the ability to suspend disbelief.) The most used argument I hear is that all living things (animals, plants, etc.) eventually die. It would seem so.

Yet death is a human idea that has been projected onto all living things. Humans are very powerful and we do create *everything* in our environment. At any rate, I won't harp on it here. Let's stick to ideas you may be more ready to accept.

Our physical condition at any point in time is completely our choice. Nothing can hurt us without our permission. That includes viruses, bacteria, toxins, and all the things you hear about in the News that are supposed to mow you down. Not without your permission!

In fact, we only show signs of aging by giving it permission. Why do we give our permission? Because we believe it's the way it has to be. Why do we believe that? Because that's the one area where everyone is taught the very same thing right from birth. Then, we see it supported as "fact" every single day.

One popular misconception is that when something seems to be wrong in the body, someone else can heal us. Even the "miracle cures" of faith healers and alternative treatments do not come from the healer or the treatment itself. The cure always comes about due to the belief and expectation of the one being healed.

In every instance, the person being healed is instructing the cells of the body to heal themselves following the treatment. If there is doubt concerning the ability of the healer or treatment to bring about the desired results, the cells will fail to receive their message to heal.

If the cells of the body are reduced to their smallest atomic component, you will find light: the universal life force. As a living entity, every cell carries every aspect of universal energy. Remember that intelligence is an aspect of that energy. In order to grasp this concept in relation to the very cells of your body, it might be useful to go back and review the principles of spirit and relate each of those principles to your cells.

We can also examine this from another angle. Personal intelligence doesn't reside in our brains. It's actually a part of our total being. The cells have inherent intelligence - and every cell is under your absolute control, waiting to do your bidding.

It's unfortunate we don't realize we are constantly talking to our cells, directing them with our thoughts and words. The thoughts and words we send them are based on our feeling-filled beliefs. Certainly we are told what our beliefs should be every day of our lives as we see and hear what goes on around us.

The moment we buy into an idea that something can hurt our bodies, we send that message to the cells. Something along the lines of, "If a certain element comes into your experience, you will bring about the condition you expect as the outcome of that element."

Since it is the cell's function to manifest your desired conditions for your own body, they follow direction perfectly. They don't make decisions regarding the basis of your beliefs, and they don't argue. They'll be more than happy to die for you if that's what you tell them to do.

Mind/Body Control

In some ways our cells are like children.

In *"How to Get Your Children to do What You Want Them to Do,"* by Paul Wood, he writes:

> *"If you want a child to practice a certain behavior, you need to tell that child, clearly and directly, exactly what to do. If you leave room for question, the child can become confused. For instance, we can't allow small children to wander into the streets and be hit by traffic. A clear and simple, 'Stay out of the street,' will tell the child exactly what to do.*
>
> *"Even adding, 'Please,' can make the statement ineffective. 'Please,' indicates that the child has a choice in the matter. Giving explanations leaves room for the child to question whether the explanation is true. Threatening also gives the child a choice. The same is true for bribing, warning and encouragement. 'I'd like for you to stay out of the street,' indicates a wish that the child may choose to grant – or not.*
>
> *"Only simple directives leave no room for question, decisions or choice. You can only give two types of directive. 'Stay out of the street,' - or – 'Don't go into the street.' The positive directive is always the most effective.*
>
> *"It's easier to get the child to begin an action – 'Play with that outside,' - rather than to stop an action – 'Don't play with that*

in the house,' – which is bringing some type of gratification. The words, *'Do not ...'* insinuate to the child that he has the option of doing the unwanted behavior. *'Stop that,'* is more effective than, *'Don't do that.'"*

So, if you want the cells of your body to behave, tell them what to do. Your clear, simple directives will have more effect than anything your cells may "hear" in the form of outside messages. It will even have more effect than the messages they receive from your unconscious mind provided you clearly intend for them to comply.

Intention is everything when it comes to your body. If you send your cells mixed signals, you'll create confusion - then it's a crap game. Directing the cells to do one thing, then allowing fear to creep in when you hear yet another report on what will kill you, is self-defeating.

When you decide to take control of your body, you must *know* you have the absolute power to do that. Sometimes, it's difficult to argue with fear messages from outside sources, especially when they are backed up by a lot of "evidence." Rather than attempt to deny any truth in the message, simply reject the concept for yourself. It may very well be true for others, but what others are willing to accept for themselves has nothing to do with you.

You may feel a little silly at first, speaking directly to the cells of your body. But, when you see how it works, you'll get over it.

Several years ago, I was preparing to move to another city. My car was in the shop being serviced, the movers were coming the next afternoon, and other things had interfered with my packing, so I was struggling to be ready on time. Suddenly I started seeing flashes of light off to the left in my peripheral vision. The flashes would come every 5 seconds or so. I had no idea what could cause that and it was very irritating.

After about three hours of this, I finally called a friend and asked if he had any ideas what could be causing such a phenomenon. He told me to go to the emergency room immediately - I had a torn retina - and I could go blind in that eye if I didn't get it corrected immediately. He also informed me the correction would require surgery. Since he wasn't a physician, I couldn't be sure he was correct but he was certainly emphatic. He even offered to drive me to the hospital, since my car wasn't available.

Luckily, he was a good enough friend to allow me to make my own decisions. I gave it about a minute's consideration and decided I didn't have time for all that. I had other things to do - things that would be very complicated to reschedule. So, instead of seeking medical attention, I sat down for a minute and spoke to the cells of my left eye.

First, I expressed sympathy that they were in distress. That effectively sent love energy to them. Then, I directed them to heal themselves. Period. I removed my attention from the eye and went about my packing. Part of me felt like we didn't have any choice in the matter, and I fully expected that eye to do exactly what I needed. It did.

Within minutes, the flashes began coming at longer and longer intervals. By the time the movers showed up the next day, I was only seeing them about once every 2 or 3 hours. By the time I reached my destination, they were completely gone, and I didn't even know when they stopped.

Several months later, I went for a routine eye exam. As the ophthalmologist examined my left eye, he asked me how long ago the surgery on my retina had been done. When I asked him what made him think I had ever had retina surgery, he told me he could see the repair.

After my explanation, he insisted a torn retina can only be repaired by surgical procedure and he had never heard of one healing without treatment. I replied I certainly had no reason to make up such a story, so I guessed he could now say he had seen a miracle. Of course, that brought on "the lecture" but it's pretty hard to argue with success.

I want to be very clear right here that I am *not* suggesting anyone else should try such a process as I used with my eye. In my case, I absolutely *knew* that eye would heal itself. There wasn't even a shadow of a doubt. But then, I have years and years of positive experiences with mind/body control.

I *never* recommend people refuse to seek medical advice. Even though we ultimately control our own healing, a physician can prepare the body for that healing. In the general population, it's faith and expectation a medical treatment will work that directs the cells to complete the job.

Everything Works Both Ways

Not only can we give direction to our body and expect the desired results - our bodies often speak to us. Stress is a result of fear - and the energies of fear interfere with our cells' ability to give optimum performance. When we begin to inflict too much stress upon our cells, they nearly always send us a message to that effect.

I was once sent a major asthma attack for just that reason. I couldn't breathe and I did see a physician. Medication relived the attacks but every time I stopped taking it, the attacks recurred. I had never had asthma in my life and couldn't believe this was happening. Finally, I realized this was simply a message from my body telling me to slow down.

I had been totally focused on a complicated project - I was pushing hard to meet a deadline - and I feared I wouldn't make the deadline. Lots of fear energy was being generated. As soon as I "heard" the message from my body, I began a relaxation technique. As I was involved with the technique, I also told my cells I had received the message, thanked them for the warning, and told them it was over. I threw out the medication - my breathing corrected itself - and I didn't have another asthma attack for almost 25 years.

Then, I had one that was caused by yet another physical condition I didn't know I had. That took a lot more energy, and a lot more overcoming of fear to get back on track to normal breathing. Yet, it was done.

The first indication of physical distress is a message from our bodies that something is interfering with their ability to work at peak levels. It's always stress of one kind or another. The cells' capacity to work for us properly is severely limited by fear energy. If we learn to pay attention to those first signals and remove the fear energy, many ailments would never expand into full-blown "dis-eases."

"Death Talk"

For some unknown reason, I once clearly "heard" something I was saying. It was utter nonsense - but it occurred to me the very cells of my body were hearing that same message. After that, I realized I needed to start listening to what comes out of my mouth. As I began to pay attention, I was amazed and appalled at the messages I'd been sending to my body.

Creating physical well-being has an added component to creating things in our outer environment. When we are creating prosperity of any other kind, our intent - whether conscious or unconscious - is of paramount importance. If we use words or have thoughts *without* intent behind them, they are basically ineffective. Casual conversation or random thoughts will not go forth to create.

When we're dealing with our physical body, intent is still very important, however, it's our intent that the cells should follow our directives. The cells *will follow any* directive, whether it is intentional or not. This is where casual conversation and random thoughts *can* become a problem.

Not only are we taught about dying from the time we're born, but we reinforce that constantly with death-talk. Everything that relates to a thought or word that our body's function should deteriorate, is accepted as a directive by the cells.

These are just a fraction of the common phrases we use on a daily basis. They come from *"Charles Fillmore's Works,"* written by Charles Fillmore, founder of the Unity Movement, in his early writings.

I thought I'd die *To my dying day*
Dead tired *Dead on my feet*
Drop dead *Kill time*
Until the day I die *This work is killing me*

Then we have the more subtle ones:

Stabbed in the back *Breaks my heart*
Cut my throat *Feeble-minded*
Shot myself in the foot *This work is crippling*
Losing my mind *Pain in the neck*
Eating away at me *Stuck in my throat*

In addition to the blatant death messages we're sending our bodies, we also send them the stressful emotional energies that lead to debilitation:

I resent that *I hate to interrupt*
I'm sorry *I envy you*
Makes me furious *I'm exhausted*
It scares me to death *I feel so guilty*

Take Action:

Make a real concentrated effort to listen to your own words for a month and you'll realize in a hurry why your body expresses certain conditions. Then, make the effort to remove these types of conversation and thought from your personal repertoire. These are habitual phrases, so they won't disappear overnight. When you catch them slipping out inadvertently, instantly reject their validity for you.

In this day of instant information, we are constantly subjected to death and dying messages. Even if you stop sending them to yourself, the media will be more than happy to send them to you. Fear sells. You may need to create new habits around what you take into your consciousness and accept for yourself. Look at it this way - it's pretty silly to accept the results of a recent study that "proves" anything - when another study will just prove it wrong in a few years anyway.

Which reminds me - have you ever considered the number of things we're told "cause" cancer? If all that is true, how does anyone live past 40? Every time we're informed of another cause of cancer, a whole new section of the population comes down with it. It will be the section that has been exposed to that "cause," - and also believes and accepts that information for themselves. The "cause" may have been there for years, but the epidemic doesn't start until the idea is implanted in the public's mind.

Would you believe me if I told you the Fountain of Eternal Youth can be found right in your own mind? How many messages do we receive, on a daily basis, telling us what to expect as the number of our years on Earth increase? I don't have to tell you what they are. I will tell you this, though - buying those "age-defying" products will only increase your belief that you need them. The only thing being defied with their use is the ability of your cells to express their true nature of life.

Even when we state our age, we state it in terms of X# of years old! In fact, why do people ever need to state their ages at all? Well, of course! So we can be categorized as to our ability! If resumes were absolutely honest - with no reference to date of birth, and people had to be hired sight unseen, we'd have a lot more experienced work force over-all. Our ability only begins to backslide because that's exactly what we expect. Tell a kid he has a low IQ - and that kid will perform at exactly the level expected.

Cell Response

Our bodies not only respond to what we tell them, they also respond to what they "see." Since our minds actually exist in every cell, the images we create in our minds are an additional message to the cells. They respond to all mind-pictures.

I have a little trick I use whenever I gain a few pounds and get uncomfortable in my clothes. Just before I go to sleep at night, I visualize myself standing in front of a mirror. The image in the mirror is me - at my preferred weight. Then, I go on to sleep and forget about it till the next night.

That's all I do. I don't get all stressed out trying to adjust my diet. That would only send fear messages. Nor do I jump up and start an exercise routine since I don't enjoy that. And, it would also create stress for me.

I don't do anything to send messages to contradict that my cells will receive the visual directive and act accordingly. They do. The extra weight magically disappears.

Athletes, actors, and sports enthusiasts have all used visual directives to improve their performance. What the cells see - they will perform. I'll probably get into trouble for saying this, but if you can believe it - and accept it for yourself - and if you are clear in your directive to your cells - you can accomplish exactly the same thing by visualizing your exercise program as you can by doing it physically.

It isn't what your cells are doing in response to the exercise - it's what you're telling them you expect of them. You can tell them you expect the same result from doing the exercise mentally - and they'll respond in the same way. Saves a heck of a lot of time too. Not to mention energy - which you could be using to produce something wonderful. Now, if you enjoy physical exercise, don't stop doing it. It's producing love energy for you.

Our bodies also appreciate and respond to natural remedies from other living cells. It isn't a good idea to introduce synthetic drugs into the body unless absolutely necessary. Many unenlightened physicians continue to deny the value of herbal remedies, mostly due to ignorance of their actual value to the human immune system.

A very few years ago, pharmaceutical companies were busy denying the effectiveness of herbal remedies for physical distress. This is no longer the case as they are now selling the very products they told us didn't work. In fact, some are now pushing for government regulation in an attempt to gain control of the markets. This will no doubt also serve to increase prices beyond anything reasonable.

No matter which way the issue swings, natural remedies will always be of the utmost value to physical well-being. Life responds to life - and herbal remedies come directly from life.

Your body also needs to be appreciated and thanked regularly for the job it does for you. Cells, like any living entity, will expand their activity (function) in response to love energy. Love is the harmonizing principle of the universe. Harmony equals balance - and balance will keep everything in perfect order.

Every time something goes "wrong" within the body, an imbalance is expressing itself. If something seems to be off balance, the cells need some loving attention. You may have noticed when I was relating my experiences in self-healing, both times, I sent love energy to those cells before issuing my directives for correction.

I will admit there have been other times when I was impatient and sent rather irritable directives. Those directives also worked - but it took more time, and the results were never quite so pleasurable as when I send the love energy.

Love energy makes everything work faster and better. It also works in more subtle ways. How often do we abuse our own bodies? That is withholding love. Are you excited about taking direction from an abusive person? Of course not.

We give love to our cells when we provide rest - care - even a proper diet. In reality, they can exist just fine without any of that. But until that becomes your truth, why not go ahead and make it easier on them? We also give love when we express appreciation. Every cell in our bodies is a living being and will always respond to appreciation.

The most important element of love you can give to your cells is discussed in the Appendix of *The MASTER COURSE*. It's a complete description of a very simple technique which should be used every day to keep your cells in top operating condition at all times.

Fulfilling Relationships

What is a "fulfilling relationship?" We have a two-fold answer to that question. When we think of "relationship," we tend to think in the narrow terms of intimate relationships. Of course our intimate relationships are a vital and important part of our lives. Yet, we actually have relationships with everyone we interact with at all - and we develop ongoing relationships, either long-term or short-term, with everyone we are involved with for specific goals.

Once you begin to accept the principles of the nature of spirit - which we all carry - you'll find even your most transient relationships begin to improve. Coming to the realization and understanding of the universal Principle of Oneness brings even more improvement.

You'll notice you no longer feel the urge to snap back at the grouchy grocery clerk. You'll have more patience when you get behind the wheel of a vehicle. You'll even begin to do those little random acts of kindness for complete strangers.

This is the result of the realization that everyone who is in front of you has an energy connection to you. It's the understanding that this person is actually a very real aspect of some part of you. When the clerk snaps, you'll be more inclined to remember the times your own grumpy mood may have affected someone else. You'll be able and willing to respond from a place of love, rather than letting it ruin your day.

Family relationships are paramount in our lives. Fulfilling relationships with family members may mean making adjustments in our interactions with family members to create more harmony in our lives. We can't just toss out our parents or siblings and replace them - no matter how dysfunctional we may believe our family is.

Once again, use of the principles will help you create more understanding relationships with those who are also physically connected to you. This, in spite of the fact that family-of-origin feelings are some of the strongest feelings we have. These are the very deepest unconscious feelings around our core beliefs that may need to be healed.

Those are the very feelings affecting all of our intimate relationships. Amazing changes begin to happen within families through the use of universal principles. Acceptance of these principles will automatically bring forgiveness in time.

First, however, it's necessary to do a thorough cleansing of the unconscious core belief feelings. We have stored so much information in our unconscious minds that, over the years, we've forgotten why we believe certain things - and we've never examined the feelings that created the beliefs in the first place.

The core belief feelings, which have been implanted with any kind of fear energy behind them, are exactly what is creating the things in our lives we do *not* want. Positive changes within the family generate new energies, which will go out and help us create the loving and lasting intimate relationships we all long for.

Choosing Intimate Relationships

People constantly look for their soul mates. Well, they're right in front of you. Every difficult relationship you ever had was with a soul mate. Perfect understanding is an aspect of a soul mate relationship. The two of you will fit together perfectly. I'll explain …

It feels like we "fall" in love: that powerful chemistry - that heart fluttering feeling - that "I've finally found it" feeling. Hold on! That isn't about love, at all! Nevertheless, we think we're in love, and all we see is the relationship made in heaven.

She is so "together" - always looks perfect and beautiful. You're so proud to be seen with her. He has that incredible mouth - you can barely take your eyes off it. It's just waiting for you to kiss. This person is so neat and tidy - such a pleasure to have around the house. Always putting things back where they belong.

Then - one - day - you wake up - and the hormones have settled down. You suddenly realize - she loves Calvin Klein or Bill Blass more than she loves you. And, he opens that incredible mouth and says something incredibly stupid. And, your "perfect" mate is so uptight you envision yourself at age 80, picking lint off the floor at gunpoint.

Welcome to the Magical Kingdom of Love! It's the only place where the beautiful princess can turn into a wicked witch - and the handsome prince can turn into a frog - overnight.

Love is definitely not blind! Love has 20/20 vision.

Those qualities driving you out of your mind are exactly the same qualities you loved so much in the beginning. You ask yourself, "How could I have missed that?" Well ... you didn't miss that. But now, your perception has changed.

How did this happen? We're looking for that "soul mate." We meet someone and there is an almost instant attraction toward each other. We feel like we've known them all of our lives. We're so comfortable with them. We each know what the other is going to say before it's said. We're sure this is the magic relationship - a true soul mate.

Well, we're absolutely right! Of *course* we know what they're going to say before they say it. Of *course* we're comfortable with them. Of *course* we feel like we've known them all our lives. We grew up with them!

This soul mate will be like one of our parents – or childhood caretakers. The one from whom we had a difficult time getting the love and understanding we needed. We always needed more to validate us from this person – and never got it. It's a soul mate alright. I repeat: Every challenging relationship is with a soul mate.

The word "soul" comes from the Greek word, "psyche" - which means "mind." - Which points to unconscious motivations. We attract - and are attracted to - another person who has our matching issues to be worked out. We come together - and we *are* soul mates. One psyche fits the other.

You may feel very much in love with this person, and you may question why you can't believe your heart. The problem is, the feelings of love being generated are left over from your past. They are actually feelings you had for your childhood caretaker.

We each carry around our own personal energy field. This field is made up of our feelings and expectations. It's generated from the core belief feelings in our unconscious minds. This energy field will reflect different energies at different times - depending on what goal we're working toward at the time.

For example, you may have a very successful career but have experienced troubled intimate relationships. If this is the case, you're radiating very different energies in your personal energy field while you are working at your job than you are when you're in a situation where a possible relationship might be established.

Whatever energies you're carrying in your personal field will move out and attract other people to you who have complementary energies. Since they do carry the complementary energy, you may also be attracted to them. The strongest attractions will be toward another who carries the particular energy surrounding your greatest need at the time.

Those raised in loving homes, with good positive relationships with their childhood caretakers, tend to have more successful relationships. They didn't feel a lack of love, and they learned to love appropriately. Therefore, they carry an energy field which projects love and is open to all possibilities of love.

People who have difficulty with intimate relationships have quite a different background. They had at least one childhood caretaker from whom they couldn't get the validation every child needs to believe they are lovable and worthy human beings. That does *not* always mean the caretaker didn't love the child.

In many cases the caretaker was simply unable to express their love in ways that were meaningful to the child. Either the child failed to receive enough positive feedback - or received too much negative feedback.

The feelings generated in this situation create the energy field surrounding us in our later intimate relationships. At the unconscious level we are still struggling to get the love we didn't perceive to be present as children. We will (again, unconsciously) seek another person with whom we might heal that earlier childhood relationship. All the while we are putting out fear energies that we may not truly be lovable.

The person we attract with those energies will be radiating energies similar to the parent/caretaker. So, we recognize them. They have the same - or similar - qualities as the caretaker. If we move into a relationship with this person, we'll end up trying to get something impossible to get - from someone who isn't capable of giving it.

Statistics show children who come from abusive homes are likely to enter abusive relationships. It's hard to believe we would walk right into such a relationship if we suffered from it as a child. A person who was abused as a child carries the energies that say, "I expect to be hurt." Those energies will, in turn, attract another person who carries energies that say, "I'm full of fury."

At the unconscious level, the formerly abused child is attracted to those rage energies. Here is a chance to work out the issues pertaining to the caretaker they felt didn't love them. Maybe they can get this new - and similar - person to love them. It makes no difference if the original abuse was physical, mental or emotional.

I've used an extreme example here but the feelings of lack of love can be from any number of situations. The caretaker who was never home - the one who was wrapped up in addictions - the one who didn't show physical affection - the one who was overly critical - the one who was completely self-involved - the one who didn't talk - or listen - to the child. Any situation where the child felt unloved - therefore unlovable.

There's a similar situation that also comes into play in building our energy fields for intimate relationships. In homes where a child learns that his parents are always at odds with each other, the child sometimes takes on responsibility for the situation. As an adult, the child expresses the characteristics of one parent - and attracts a person very much like the other parent - in an effort to work out those parental problems.

How many times have you said, "She or he is exactly like my mother/father!" The child can take on the characteristics of either parent - regardless of gender. People who go through life with serial marriages are often switching back and forth - playing the roles of first one parent, then the other. Each time with a person who has the appropriate energies to fulfill the other role.

Why do we long for the person of our dreams, then go right out and choose the person of our worst nightmare? First of all, we don't recognize we're doing it. It's all unconscious. The energy of the feelings we have about our past relationships, with the people we depended on for our very existence, is creating the energy we put into the universe. It has to find a complementary energy. Then, the energy of feelings we have from any past failed relationships of our own is added to that - reinforcing it - and making it even stronger.

Is there any hope? Of course! We can make different decisions. Once we have examined the workings of our unconscious feelings, through self-analysis, we can replace those feelings through exercises such as I've provided in *The MASTER COURSE* Workbook, *"Who's Driving Your Bus?"*

CREATING YOUR FULFILLING RELATIONSHIP

It's entirely possible to create the relationship of your dreams. Universal Law: everything works both ways. If you've created one kind of relationship - you can just as easily create the other.

When we use creative processes consciously, we take control of energy and bring what we want into our lives. But first, a word of caution ... Even after you effectively heal your personal energy field, you must remember one critical point. *Never, ever, set your sights on starting a new relationship with a particular person!*

Some students who come to me are not only wishing to create a fulfilling relationship - but a relationship with a particular person. This is one of the biggest mistakes anyone can make! It can also be one of the most sorrowful.

When we are attracted to a particular person as a candidate for a lasting intimate relationship, we need to understand it isn't that person we truly want. What we want is the kind of relationship we picture ourselves having with that person. As in all areas of creation, we must be very clear as to our intent. What is the very foundation of the desire? It's that *fundamental* desire we must create to fulfill our longing.

One of the most difficult concepts to teach students is that they will create *exactly* what they ask for. That makes it entirely possible to bring a particular person into a relationship with you. However, why would you want to limit the universe?

It's the loving relationship you want. It's very likely you will bring the person you think you want to you. Only to find out later that this person isn't capable - or willing - to have the kind of relationship you had envisioned with them.

If you are attracted to a certain person and that person doesn't seem to be interested enough in you to come to you on their own, the complementary energies are missing. Now, assuming you have healed your own energy fields, and you are radiating only energies of love - you definitely want to attract complementary energies. And, you will!

If your chosen someone isn't responding to those love energies, they are still tied up in their own fear issues. They will only be interested in someone they perceive to have those same kinds of issues. Be forewarned. If you are able to bring this person into a relationship with you in spite of all that - the relationship *will not last!* And, it may leave you in a crumpled heap wondering why this creative stuff doesn't work. It does work - but each of us is responsible for choosing wisely.

Believe it or not each of us could be happy with many different people. There isn't just one special person who can fulfill our relationship desires. Nothing is a waste of time. We learn from every encounter. But, it's still in your own best interests to take positive action and use creative techniques to connect with someone right for you.

Take control of your life. This is too big a decision to leave to "fate." Fate can kick your ol' wazoo. Decide and create. You will be empowered by the very fact that you're doing it.

In general, you will be able to create the kind of intimate relationships you desire when you begin to love yourself as you wish to be loved. This comes after working through the unconscious core belief feelings regarding to your own personal worth. It will come when you accept every part of yourself. How many times have you heard "Love your neighbor as yourself?"

The truth is, we can only love others in the same degree that we can love ourselves. At the spirit level of our consciousness (superconscious) we *know* of our connection with *all* life. Therefore, what we consciously judge in ourselves - we judge in others. And vice versa.

It's imperative we understand our feelings and own them. It's downright scary how many women are walking around creating this very reality when they say, "All men are _____." (You fill in the blank.)

Using the proper tools of self-analysis, many of these women would find they accepted certain beliefs because - it's what their mothers told them! Same situation with men whose fathers taught them, "Men have to be tough!" Or, whatever.

Owning your own feelings means you must find out what *you* actually believe. As you start to recognize how your beliefs are self-fulfilling prophesies, take the time to examine where you got them. Who said so? Have you been acting on the beliefs of another - bringing *their* beliefs and issues into your own life?

How many concepts have been shoved down your throat as "right" when they're not right for you at all? We each must be very honest with ourselves and begin to accept our own truths. What do you believe? What are you comfortable with? When you can do that, you'll find tremendous power in saying, "This is who *I* am - and *this* is what I want."

Then, you have the absolute power to create exactly what makes you happy. More importantly, your changes in perception will allow you to keep it until you decide to create something else.

To increase love for ourselves can only make us more loving. We learn to judge behavior rather than people. As we grow more loving, we attract more loving people. We do have to open our hearts with total honesty. With acceptance of ourselves, the love energy flows out and attracts a like energy.

Recognizing the Real Thing

How we can recognize if it's the "real thing" when we begin developing deep feelings for someone? There's no answer to "how" because the only answer is - we can't. Relationships are made - not born. Yes, even the bad ones. It takes time to know if a relationship is going to be what you'd like it to be. I can, however, show you how it should look from the beginning.

Entering into a relationship in an effort to fulfill something you think you don't have just won't work! Believing another person will make you complete is doomed to failure. We have to work through our own issues and come to a place of being a whole, emotionally healthy, person within ourselves. Only then will we attract other whole, emotionally healthy, people.

The kind of committed relationship many people only dream of is easily defined. It consists of two whole, and emotionally healthy, people coming together to form a greater unit. That greater unit is the relationship itself. The relationship becomes an entity unto itself. Decisions are based, not on what is best for one partner or the other - but on what is best for the relationship itself.

It also does help to have somewhat similar backgrounds and experiences. This is often needed for understanding and ongoing support.

In many good relationships the partners appear to be opposites in every way. If it's a fulfilling relationship, both partners are usually expressing what the other isn't expressing - but what they both have. This isn't from need, but from a sense of balance. People in healthy relationships are never totally opposite, nor are they ever completely the same. It's as if each is the other side of the same coin.

Some general work can be done that will help you in creating your own intimate relationship. This should be done with forethought - preferably after cleaning up the feelings of the core beliefs in the unconscious. You'll find what you want in a relationship is likely to change, once you change some of your erroneous beliefs.

Take Action:

Make a list of qualities you'd like your significant other to have. Write down everything you can think of. Then, one by one, honestly answer the question of whether you have these same qualities. Be sure your wants are wants - and not needs.

If you don't have the qualities you're looking for in another, you're looking for someone to make you complete. Another person can never do that for you. The fulfilling relationship may make your life complete - but it can never do your personal healing for you.

Secondly, check your levels of the qualities you desire in another and get clear on the levels you'd like to see. For instance, you may have a good sense of humor and would like the other person to also have that quality. But, could you deal with someone who spends every Saturday afternoon watching The 3 Stooges on TV, leg slapping and laughing like a hyena? Be honest.

As with all creative projects, we must have clear intent concerning what we want. Do your own personal self-analysis; heal your own fears. Learn to accept the universal principles, then use them in a positive way. Do the head-work. Think your desires through carefully. Ask yourself questions and don't give up until you get the true answers.

What we want most is for someone to really know us - and accept us as we are. We must be willing to do the same. Accept love as a celebration of humanness - not perfection. Each person is a very unique human being. People are fascinating - keep an open mind. But, know what you're looking for. *Then* - trust your heart.

The Road to Transformation

You've heard it a thousand times: do whatever and "change your life." So you do whatever it is and maybe change happens. Maybe it doesn't. The absolute worst is when you do manage to bring about change - only to lose whatever was gained down the line.

This is what makes *The MASTER COURSE* different. Change isn't enough. It takes more than a few processes to bring about permanent change. It's only an adjustment in perspective that brings lasting transformation. I hope, after being exposed to the basic principles of universal energy, you'll make the choice for transformation.

In order to assist you even further in this endeavor, I'd like to introduce you to the three levels of consciousness. These are the levels of awareness each of us has within our conscious minds. Each level is an increase in our realization of certain universal truths. As we grow in awareness, we move through the stages until we reach the highest level. I call this transition "The Evolution of Consciousness."

Physical Consciousness

Those in this first stage of consciousness are intent upon meeting their physical needs. The most basic needs of food, water and safety must be met before a human can even begin to develop capacities in other areas. Once those needs are met, the needs expand to include a source of monetary income. We also search for loving attachments in our need for community.

Each person at this level will determine for themselves what they believe is mandatory for their existence. Situations in the outer world of each will tend to shape this consciousness. These people are often driven by a motivation stemming from feelings of deprivation. There never seems to be enough to provide - or sustain - a feeling of physical welfare.

When living in this consciousness, people tend to place blame when they feel their needs aren't being met. They may believe life is controlled by a rigid, uncaring, or even vengeful, God. Or, they may believe life is controlled by fate - or is simply a random, accidental process.

Persons stuck in this consciousness feel helpless due to their inability to control their material world. It also indicates a type of irresponsibility regarding their innate power. Power is relinquished to outside forces.

In working with people involved in the process of consciousness-raising, I've observed a definite growth course that begins with some type of perceived deprivation at the physical/material level. Change is desired due to lack of health, wealth or happiness.

These people tell me they feel out of control and powerless in some area of life. If there is a belief in any kind of "higher power," it's often a God "out there" who for his own reasons is punishing them - or simply doesn't care. They usually believe situations, other people, or society as a whole is causing their pain.

They feel "stuck" - in the pain of a paralysis that won't allow them to overcome their challenges. This very pain - and a feeling of desperation - will often drive those stuck in this consciousness to seek assistance and finally begin to move toward the next level.

Psychic Consciousness

The word "psychic" often gives an image of one who is extremely intuitive and adept at extrasensory perception (ESP). For our purposes, however, it is used - according to its true definition - to indicate "mind."

At this level of consciousness people learn to use the power of the mind. They acknowledge the energies of feelings (energies that exist behind words and thoughts) and use these energies to manifest desires. People take control of their lives through techniques such as affirmations, visualization, meditation and thought conditioning. They also see how these processes are actually an aspect of nature.

Those who are in psychic consciousness have a realization of the relationship between our inner and outer worlds. They gain understanding of how we project our own life experience. A sense of control is gained as people learn to bring positive situations into their own lives.

A belief develops in some kind of universal power. This power may, or may not be called "God." As these techniques begin to produce the desired results, they soon understand the power is coming from within, since this where they believe our minds reside. Some form of meditation is usually learned during the time of psychic consciousness. It comes about from the necessity of having quiet time when using universal energies for creation.

Whether it is termed "psychic" or not, this is the consciousness usually achieved by those who take responsibility for creating their own lives through the manipulation of universal energies. As they accept that universal laws actually exist, they use that power to their own ends, healing whatever outer condition set them on this consciousness-raising path in the first place. Now, material desires can be achieved. Deprivation is ended.

Many people who achieve this second level of consciousness consider themselves to be highly spiritual. If that's the case, they will move on to the next level with relative ease. However, it isn't necessary to have any degree of spirituality at all in psychic consciousness. The energies don't require that. They may be used for any purpose - even purposes which others might judge as "wrong." The energies tapped into at psychic consciousness are completely neutral and always work with the correct manipulation.

Spiritual Consciousness

Spiritual consciousness calls for developing a conscious connection with the foundation of a universal spirit. This universal spirit may be called by many names. None is more correct than any other. It's all related to the universal creative source. This connection is nearly always achieved through the use of deep meditation.

The transition from psychic to spiritual consciousness is often so subtle it goes unrecognized until it is nearly complete. While still in psychic consciousness, many students will naturally move into deeper meditative practices. As these people become more adept at deep meditation, they begin to have a feeling of their minds expanding.

They now sense the power is not only within them, but they are within the power. This brings about the realization - and experience - of universal mind, which in turn, brings about spiritual consciousness.

At the level of spiritual consciousness, we grasp that the universal spirit - or power - can *only* be good and must be used lovingly and in a *giving*, rather than *receiving*, manner. We cease using the power and allow the power to use - and work through - us. We stop making things happen - instead, we begin allowing things happen - with the full knowledge that all things work for good. When this level is reached, we gain more than we had ever hoped for when material need was the motivation.

Spiritual consciousness is not necessary for creating the life of your desires. It may, or may not, come about for you naturally as you become adept at using universal energies. If it does come about, it will come easily - and be in the form of a deep inner knowing. It isn't necessary to struggle to reach it.

On the other hand, if this is a consciousness you would prefer not to reach - no problem. Your intent will settle the matter in exactly the manner you prefer.

Moving Forward

As life on this planet becomes increasingly complicated, people long, more and more, for security. Many don't know how to get off the fast track long enough to remember what security is - much less sit in silence to find it. They are quite accustomed to structuring every moment of the day. They seem to cling even tighter to absolute structure in their personal lives, as things around them appear to be changing at impossible rates of speed.

This clinging to something with which we are familiar can become chaotic in its extreme - and life feels out of control. Feelings of being unable to cope with things "out there" show little understanding of responsibility. Severe deprivation in some area, along with a feeling of helplessness is the ultimate result. Seen in the light of "all things work for good," this deprivation prepares one to begin seeking alternative methods for coping with life.

When an evolution of consciousness begins, order will ultimately be restored. As we begin to comprehend the use of universal energies at the psychic level of consciousness, we also begin to accept 100% responsibility for our own lives. In addition, we learn at this level that we receive what we give - and a sense of control is established.

Spiritual consciousness, in turn, must be achieved by letting go completely of the need to "get" by simply *receiving* all things - and giving what is received to others. Until one learns how to "get" through psychic consciousness, we cannot transcend to receiving greater good through greater giving.

The road to transformation is a path from helplessness - to control - to surrender. With few exceptions, it is nearly impossible to move from helplessness to the surrender necessary for spiritual consciousness without first experiencing some degree of control. That's why it's so important to learn to use creative techniques properly.

When we reach this point of surrender, we stop using all processes and creative techniques. They are no longer necessary since we can now instantly accept whatever is needed in the moment.

Spiritual consciousness is the source of all things. It's the realization of our eternal connection in Oneness - and of the reality that we are each directly connected to - and a part of - the universal creative source.

Those who achieve spiritual consciousness have all things as they are accepted. Most importantly, we ultimately accept the truth that, indeed, Body, Mind, and Spirit are One.

At that point - Transformation is Complete.

I can't stress enough that this lesson is the most important lesson in the Course. You must accept these concepts, and take them deeply within yourself. Every technique you'll learn in the Course rests upon your acceptance of these principles. They are the foundation upon which your transformation rests.

It's possible you may find yourself a bit uncomfortable with the spiritual concepts involved in this lesson. Please rest assured, they are *spiritual* concepts and work with every religion. You will never be asked to change your religious beliefs.

Again, I caution you to be patient. It takes time to internalize everything you'll learn here. Please read this lesson, in its entirety, at least once a day for the next 30 days. It's also very important for you to continue to work with the Workbook as frequently as possible.

Part Two

PART TWO

Introduction to Part Two

By now, I hope you've thoroughly familiarized yourself with Part One of this book. From this point on - if you have any difficulty with the techniques - go back and read it again. Read it over and over and over. Part One is intended to help you change the necessary general mind-sets.

It isn't something you can read once and say, "Okay, I understand." You need to read it *deeply!* By that I mean, you need to think about everything you read and see how it might apply to your individual life. In fact, each time you review Part One, you'll have additional insights. Part One is the basis of the entire *MASTER COURSE*. Everything else builds on it.

I mention this now as a reminder. If, at any time, you begin to feel "lost" in the techniques, go back to Part One. It probably means you've forgotten some very basic premise of the entire procedure.

From this point on, we'll be applying the mind-sets. I'd like you to remember it's pretty difficult to read a couple of books and instantly turn into a life magician. Everything must be *practiced*. Remember, you crawled before you walked - and walked before you ran. You didn't become mobile overnight.

In Part Two there will be more for you to do. Rather than making this part 10 long chapters, it is divided into many short sub-chapters. This will make it very easy for you to find what you need easily when you wish to review. Each point that needs consideration is in its own section.

Spend as much time as possible on the "Take Action" sections. After you've done them for a while, be sure to re-read them to be sure you haven't fallen into any bad habits. Try to understand the function of each action so you'll know what you are trying to achieve.

If you haven't already created the exact life you want, it means you've been creating something else. We constantly create our lives, whether we mean to or not. You already have lots of experience in creating your life! Re-training is going to be necessary to begin creating the life you really want.

I've had students come to me and say, "I've read every book ever written on how to create a successful life. I already know *how* it's done but it isn't working for me!"

Let me assure you right now that "knowing how it's done" and applying what you know are two very different things. We must be willing to tear down the old before we can build the new.

Read every chapter of *The MASTER COURSE*, whether it's what you want to manifest or not. Nearly all techniques are interchangeable. Just the little detail you need may be found in a chapter on a different subject than what you are interested in creating.

Yes, But ...

How many times do you think you might have talked yourself right out of something you wished to create with, "Yes, but ...?" It happens all the time. Even to some who are experienced in using universal energy to create their desires.

Perhaps you have decided you *will* bring about transformation in some area of your life. You may use any - or all - of the creative techniques you ever heard about. Your desire is deep. You have managed to generate lots of positive feeling about it. You have remembered it is the energy behind our feelings that goes out into the universe to attract like energies. You remember this is what actually causes the desire to manifest into being. Everything seems exactly right. You *know* it's going to work for you!

And then - it happens. You hear that sneaky little voice in the back of your head say, "Yes, but ... what if I'm not good enough to have that?" "Yes, but ... what if I'm not *supposed* to have that?" "Yes, but ... what if I did something wrong in the creative process?" "Yes, but ... what if something stands in my way?" "Yes, but ..." "Yes, but ..." "Yes, but ..."

Well yes, but ... *nuts* to that! That nasty little voice has a name. And, you have met fear many times.

The only creative feeling energy stronger than fear is love. No matter how many processes you use - or how perfectly you use them - once fear creeps in, it will take complete control of the creative process. It will bring about the very thing you fear, which in this instance, is you won't get what you want.

I've even seen people, who are very experienced in using positive creative process go so far as to create exactly what they want. Then, turn around and say, "Yes, but ... what if I can't do it again?"

In the words of author, Richard Bach:

> *"Argue for your limitations, and sure enough, they're yours."*

Take Action:

Begin now to put love in place of fear. Love yourself enough to know - you are always good enough - you are supposed to have everything good. You can't do anything wrong when you create everything from a place of love - and everything will get out of your way to bring you peace and happiness.

Every day for the next 30 days, watch your thoughts carefully. Begin to replace old ideas with these true concepts. Remind yourself on a daily basis. When ideas to the contrary come up, replace them immediately with the truth: you are good enough!

Living With Fear

Living with fear? Why would we want to live with fear? The answer is - we don't. The rest of the answer is - we always will. I didn't say, "Live *in* fear" - I said, "Live *with* it." Might as well get used to the idea.

In today's society we are bombarded with fear messages - constantly. In fact, they've been aimed at us ever since the day we were born. That isn't going to change very soon. Fear sells. Count the fear messages on tonight's newscast. Unless you plan to completely isolate yourself from all media - worrisome friends - and let's not forget the family that terrorizes you daily - you will have to learn to live with fear.

Many students believe they must completely eliminate fear in order to create the lives they desire. Not true - and it can't be done. If it were true, nobody would ever create anything positive. If you'll look closely at your fears, you'll find many of them don't even belong to you. They belong to whoever is trying to sell you on them. They have nothing to do with what you can create.

How many times have you heard, "All we have to fear is fear itself?" That's an absolute truism. Fear is a feeling. Feeling is energy. Energy creates. To deny fear simply pushes that energy deep into your psyche where it can do its dirty work. Better to acknowledge fear and deal with it. When fear rears its ugly head - examine it. Does it even make sense for you? Is it yours?

Treat fear like what it is. Energy. Acknowledge that it is present - then decide for yourself whether it applies to you. Fear is the culprit that causes us to forget who we are. Let that energy move right through you - and keep on going. Focus your intent on what you want. Not on what you fear. Your intent will make the final call.

Fear is always transmuted by love. Know who you are! Love yourself enough to stand up to fear. Live with it if you must - don't live in it!

Take Action:

You may or may not decide to work with this action technique. If you choose not to do it now - you may change your mind later.

Pay attention to everything going on around you that generates fear. Then decide what you can eliminate. You may not wish to give up television - but you might decide to choose your programs more carefully. You may have fear-mongering friends who need to be seen less often - if at all. What do you read? What kind of movies to you see?

Replace these activities with other activities and people who are uplifting and positive. You do not need to allow fear into your personal space. It's your space - you have the choice. We can at least live with as little fear as possible.

A Matter of Resistance

It's an interesting phenomenon that the things we tend to resist most, often turn out to be the very things that move us forward with the greatest power. It definitely bears thinking about.

A student once said to me, "When I look back over my life, it seems like the worst things that ever happened to me - turned out to be the best things that ever happened to me. Why does it work out like that?"

The answer is this. The "worst things that ever happen" are only judged to be "bad" by our unfounded ideas of what life will be like if a certain situation comes into being. Always a situation we believe we don't want. We have preconceived ideas that we wouldn't like that situation one bit.

What makes it the "worst thing" is simply our resistance to it. We imagine horrible pain of one kind or another if a certain situation comes to pass. Then, in the manner of self-fulfilling prophesy, we feel that pain even before the anticipated event occurs. It's the anticipation of the feared event that makes it even more painful if it does happen.

Take Action:

Look back through your life and remember things that happened which felt like "the worst thing that could happen." Then move forward in your memory to identify what came later. You'll nearly always find something wonderful that could never have come about if "the worst thing that could happen" hadn't happened!

Our greatest lessons for growth - and moving forward toward a more positive lifestyle - are in the areas of our greatest resistance. *The pain lives only in the resistance.*

Building Commitment

I received some email from readers of one of my columns who all had the same comment - and, the same question. Since I know that when some ask - others are also wondering, I'll answer the question for everyone in this Course. The following paragraph is the issue in question.

"The first thing that will guarantee your ultimate success is the primary thing required for all successful creation. Commitment. You must make a total commitment to your own transformation. Until you do that, it's just too easy to turn back - or give up. You are completely ineffective without commitment."

The gist of the writer's comments were that they had, at some point in time, committed to creating to a particular situation - yet, they were still ineffective. The question was, "How do I know when I have the full commitment it takes for success?"

The Answer:

Although you must clearly state your intent for creating your desire, making the commitment takes more than stating your intent. Intent is part of the commitment. The commitment - and the intent itself - comes first. The *statement* of intent sends the energy of the commitment out into the universe to create.

Making a statement without the full energy of true commitment is ineffective. That's one reason why affirmations so often fail. The intense desire (feeling) of commitment must be behind the statement. The repetition of hypnotic statements has no energy.

How do you know when you're fully committed? It's an internal feeling. Deep inside. You *know!* You know you will not accept anything less than that to which you are committed. Period! Does it take determination? You bet! Allow doubt to creep in, and you are bound to let fear slip out to create what you do not want.

If you have faced this particular challenge of doubt, most likely some of your negative core belief feelings are standing in the way of true commitment. This is why I highly recommend you work continually through *The MASTER COURSE* Workbook, *"Who's Driving Your Bus?"* Those negative core belief feelings will win out every time - until you change them. Change your core belief feelings, and you will always be capable of the true commitment needed for creating your desires.

Take Action:

Begin with baby steps. Find something you want to do - something you know you can do. Set your intent by making a commitment to do it by a certain time. State your intent with feeling.

Now - notice the feelings you have about this matter. You already know you can do it so you will be able to examine what true commitment "feels" like. No doubt exists in this feeling.

Later, you will be able to bring about this feeling at will. Right now, I'd just like for you to become very familiar with it so you'll know later what you're aiming for.

The Power of Silence

I sat at my keyboard one morning, waiting to be inspired with some sage advice for a weekly column. I waited - and I waited - and I waited. Nothing. I looked outside into the yard. Nature is always a source of inspiration but nothing caught my eye.

Finally, I succumbed to the urge to "get on my own case." Why hadn't I followed my usual habit and written this last night? Why had I waited until the noises and bustling energies of the day were all around me? Aha! At last! That's the very point.

When we're involved with the deliberate creation of positive adjustments for our lives, we need "clean" energy. We can achieve that by going high into the mountains. Yet, that isn't an option for everyone. Rather, we spend our days surrounded by toxic energies of traffic, sirens, the media hawking their scandal sheets and fear mongering. Those toxic energies can interfere with the clarity needed for creation.

When we decide to create something new for ourselves, we first need to listen to the "still small voice" within. In fact, it's that inner voice that prompts us to the need for change. Then - if we listen - it will show us the divine direction for our path. Divine direction being the very best way to accomplish what is perfect for our lives.

Secondly, we will need to send the appropriate inner energies out into the universe to create our intentions. It helps to have a clear path. Don't make those energies fight their way through the chaos of our busyness.

Think about setting aside some quiet time each day for calling upon your creative energies. If necessary, choose a time very late at night - or very early in the morning. A time of little sound. A time of little motion. Here is where you'll find your most powerful connection - with your innermost self - and with the universal energies of life.

Take Action:

Make a habit of connecting with the creative energies of the universe at least once every day - in the silence. This is very important! You don't even need to try to create anything at this point. Just become used to the energies of silence flowing around and through you.

Keeping Quiet

One of the secrets of successful creation for any part of your life is just that. A secret. It's a secret between you and your inner-most self.

Taking control of life requires us to absolutely know we have the power to do so. As you create the changes leading to transformation - in any area of life - you must control those energies that will affect your creation. You can do that! You may know that for yourself - but do your family and friends believe it? For the most part: probably not.

Let's assume you're in the midst of attracting more abundant wealth to yourself. You are generating the positive feelings that will go out into the universe and create wealth for you. You're feeling constant, happy expectancy as you go about using the creative techniques.

Then, you tell someone close to you what you're up to. If the other person doesn't also believe 100% you will accomplish your goal, negative energies will start being generated around you. The negative feedback will steal into your consciousness - raising doubts, based in fear of failure.

Fear of failure is the biggest single obstacle in using creative processes of any kind. It can creep in at any time, even without other people adding to it. We can learn to change our thoughts quickly when this happens, but we do not need the added burden of constantly needing to overcome the doubts of other people close to us.

Often, a person you confide in will attempt to give you verbal support. Yet, they may have serious doubts about your power to create what you want. They might as well have said so - because you will read their internal negative energies anyway.

If others are allowed to create any doubt whatsoever in your ability to have what you want, you will have to expend part of your energy overcoming the fear energies of that doubt. Don't do it! Keep your creative activities strictly to yourself! Then you have absolute control over the energies surrounding your project.

Do not dilute the positive energies of your creative plan by sharing that plan with others. The exception to this, of course, would be if you are totally "in synch" with another and you are both working on a creative project together.

Energy of Life

CREATIVE energies can be either positive or negative. Since the meanings of the words "positive" and "negative" are subjective - dependent upon who is deciding - I like to use the words "harmonious" and "inharmonious" to describe their meaning to any particular person.

For our purposes in the Course, however, we will use "positive" and "negative." Bear in mind "positive" means anything that is happy - or love-filled - to you. "Negative" means anything that causes you pain or creates fear.

The positive creative energies are the energies of life. The negative creative energies are the energies of "death." They take away from life in some manner.

Although you create the energy fields around you with your words, thoughts, and beliefs - you also have universal energies around you at all times. These are the energies of absolute good and they should be used to the maximum.

The more ancient cultures of our planet seemed to have a better grasp of working with energy than our more modernized societies. Different cultures have different ways of working with these energies. The basic premise is always the same - but the disciplines may be different.

The ancient Chinese art of Feng Shui (pronounced "fong-shway" or sometimes "fung-shwee") teaches using energies in an appropriate manner to affect balance and order in your surroundings. With balance and order, you will only create using the most positive energies. Feng Shui involves working with ch'i (pronounced "chee"), which is the energy of life.

You can find many good books on this art of balance, so I don't attempt to teach it in *The MASTER COURSE*. Feng Shui, however, involves some very basic principles that I feel everyone should be aware of - and use. It isn't necessary to go deeply into Feng Shui if you're not comfortable with it. Some people consider it to be superstition. But, I'm here to tell you - *it works!*

The most basic principles are necessary if you hope to make use of the most positive universal energies for the creation of your desires.

First, you will need to be sure the environment where you spend your time is sparkling clean. This is especially true for windows. You want the positive universal energies to flow freely all around you. Bright, or light-reflecting objects, such as mirrors and lights, reflect the energy - keeping it more intense.

Moving objects, such as mobiles or fountains keep the energy moving and heavy objects are used for grounding. The energy of life is important and is brought in objectively with plants, flowers, fish - anything "alive."

Both colors and sounds carry certain energies. You know this by the feelings evoked in you when you are surrounded by certain colors or sounds. Before you blow this idea off - think about that. Does a certain color irritate you - or make you feel peaceful? Do you prefer certain types of music to others? Of course! You are reacting to the energies of those particular colors or those particular musical tones.

Rather than attempt to teach you the art of Feng Shui (which you can learn in many other places) I simply want you to consider how you might keep positive energy around you. What makes you feel happy? What makes you feel alive? *Feelings create!*

The main thing is to keep your environment open, uncluttered, clean and attractive. And, I mean attractive to you! Never mind what your neighbors think. It's your life you are creating here. Whatever makes you happy and comfortable is right for you.

Before we leave this subject, I want to mention one more thing. It's important that everything around you is in good working order. If it doesn't work - either get it fixed or get rid of it! You can't create the necessary harmonious atmosphere if everything isn't working with you rather than against you.

Replace that cracked window - and repair the leaky facet or the running toilet. Which, by the way, in Feng Shui represents your wealth being drained away from you! Re-circulating water, such as a fish tank or a fountain, re-circulates those same wealth energies. This represents exactly what you will learn to do with money. Keep it circulating.

Take Action:

We do this exercise in many different ways - and usually many times. Start now to pay attention to your environment. Is it drab - or is it alive? Does it seem as if energy can flow freely? Most importantly - are you comfortable in it? Does it feel like a happy place? Begin to make small changes, then see what feelings they invoke in you.

Prosperity and Wealth

Is there a difference between "prosperity" and "wealth?" You bet there is! You can be monetarily wealthy - and still not be prosperous. Prosperity indicates an over-all prosperous life. It includes peace, health, fulfilling relationships - of all kinds - and plenty of money. Many very wealthy people don't have all this. Using the entire *MASTER COURSE* effectively will provide all these things. Prosperity.

Now - having said all that, we're going to address the thing most people seem to want most. The thing people feel most deprived of - most in lack of - is money. For the purposes of these chapters on wealth, we'll stick to material wealth. You'll pick up the other areas of prosperity in other chapters.

Obviously money isn't everything. Yet, I'm the first to say that, "Contrary to popular opinion, money can buy a heck of a lot of happiness." Anyone who doesn't believe that should try living without it for a while. In the words of Maye West, "I've been both rich - and I've been poor. Rich is better!"

You must go through four very distinct stages when creating wealth. People have found themselves wealthy without doing any of this consciously. Yet, at some level - and in some way - it was done.

We are going to cover these stages in Parts Two through Three. In Part Four, we'll pull it all together with the added processes that will guarantee success. Each stage takes some time. Rushing through the stages to get to the pot of gold at the end of the rainbow simply won't work. In fact, it will slow you down in the long run.

Give yourself time. Work on these ideas every day. Make them a very real part of your daily life. You may have a lot of bad habits to change, and you can't change a habit overnight. If fact, habits will fight to stay alive. You may have to go through a few uncomfortable moments to eradicate old habits and develop new ones.

Expect to succeed using the techniques presented in *The MASTER COURSE*. Expectation is a powerful drawing mechanism. It will help you to control your thoughts. Thoughts are energy and interact with other energies to bring about desires. The power of a made up mind is awesome in its ability to produce exactly the results you have decided.

Mental Consciousness

At first, we are going to be working with "mental-consciousness." The law of mind action is just another term for the universal law of cause and effect. Which is what we use to bring all things into our lives. It's how we get the things we want. It's also how we get most of the things we *don't* want!

This law must be used very carefully. Because it always works! Every time! Remember - we attract into our lives what we think about - and talk about - with feeling. We can also bring in what someone else has told us we would because we believed it. Belief is a feeling.

Let's go over a couple of things. We need to set aside some erroneous beliefs about trying to create wealth.

First, understand that old tapes - old beliefs you have about yourself - can determine what you manifest in life. The tapes I'm talking about here are rarely of a positive nature. Usually they come from childhood - but not always. They need to be cleaned out and discarded.

Old memories are full of emotion. Emotion is feeling. Feeling creates. You must begin defining yourself for yourself. Don't allow other people to tell you who you are. You need to get to the realization of who you truly are.

Take Action:

Begin now to test the idea that "thoughts held in mind, produce after their kind." This is the basic premise of mental-consciousness. Think of something you would like to accomplish or have. Start small.

Now - hold that thought. "See" it in your mind exactly the way you would like for it to be. Every time you think of it - stop and picture your desired outcome.

If a fear thought creeps in - don't panic. Simply replace the fear thought with your perfect mental image. Do it calmly and firmly.

Don't be overly concerned with fear thoughts at first. They are part of old habits and conditioning. Becoming afraid they will wipe out your creation will do nothing but add more fear energy. Just gently remove those thoughts and replace them. Tell yourself, "I have no need of this," and banish the thought.

Remember Who You Are

You were never intended to have anything other than absolute good in your life. *Believe* you are worthy of every good thing. If you don't accept it - you'll never see it.

You may have to do some work on this. Dump the guilt. Dump the shame. Dump the fear. I know that seems easier said than done. Yet, it's easier than you think. As always - it takes commitment on your part.

The following exercise was mentioned in the previous chapter. Here it is given as an actual action technique in more detail. This particular technique has many, many uses. Its value is without bounds. Here, we are using it to recondition your feelings about yourself.

Take Action:

Start paying attention to your thoughts on a daily basis. When unworthy thoughts about yourself come up - reject them. Look at each thought objectively - with as little feeling as possible - and understand they are false beliefs. Then, reject them. You have no need for them!

Now, use one of the most valuable affirmations. Tell yourself, "I AM finished with this." Then, let it go. Say it firmly - and say it only one time - then turn your thoughts to something you see as positive about yourself. You are redirecting your thoughts!

Don't deny you ever heard these things - or claim they have no effect on you. They most definitely had an effect on you or your conscious mind wouldn't believe you. The creative channel we call the "subconscious mind" will not deliver what the conscious mind doesn't accept and believe.

Simply reject these unworthy thoughts and beliefs through non-attention. We dissolve energies through non-attention. Turn your attention to the absolute truth of who you truly are - a part of the perfect universal life force. Start with that - and *hold to this truth!*

We also need to understand that creating your own life does not mean you can cause other people to do your bidding. I'd like to urge you to think very carefully before you try to manifest anything in your life that requires a certain response from a particular person. If someone owes you money, don't try to mentally "force" that person to pay you.

Don't get your control issues going on this thing. It's very tempting to do that sometimes. Just go for what is best for your life - and leave those other people alone. You'll be proud of yourself for doing it. You will have the universe at your command. You don't need another person to do your bidding.

Fear of Economic Insecurity

There's one more thing that stands in the way of creating wealth - and it's a big one. Fear of economic insecurity will stop you in your tracks. I can tell you how to get over it in two words. *Get rich!*

That seems like the logical solution but, of course, it isn't. And, all the reasons I've already mentioned, concerning your beliefs about your worthiness to be rich. Many, many people, once they do have financial wealth, then proceed to start worrying about losing it.

That's one of the reasons so many people run out and buy lottery tickets when the payout gets up to 100 million dollars. They figure they can't possibly lose 100 million dollars. And besides, they're probably going to receive it in increments. So, they can't lose it, right? Wrong! A person with a poverty-consciousness can lose 100 *billion* dollars through the very fear of the loss.

If we sense a monetary lack - we have a poverty-consciousness. This means that we "think poor." Where did it originate? The same place most other erroneous beliefs come from - learned behavior.

We weren't born worrying about whether we would be fed. But, if we weren't fed - we learned to worry about it. It's all in our memory banks.

"Turn off the lights! Do you think we own the electric company?"

"No, we can't afford it."

"Shut the door! Heat costs money!"

"You can't have everything you want!"

And, my personal favorite - from one of my grandmothers:

"You don't need any more than two squares of toilet paper. It's expensive!"

My brother and I were Charmin thieves before we were 5 years old!

So, that "stuff" is in your mind's memory, and it has formed habit patterns and false beliefs about scarcity. We need to bring all that right up - look at it - and then **discard it**! It keeps us believing there isn't enough. If we don't re-think some of these things, we'll keep right on acting from a place of lack. Even when we know there is enough!

Do you happen to have a sack or box full of used gift bows put away someplace? Or worse, do you keep wrinkled wrapping paper? Do you have old frayed shirts that are "good enough to wear around the house?" Do you really need to save those things? As adults, it's our responsibility to adjust those childhood limits. Throw that used gift-wrapping - and those old shirts - out!

> *If you have a poverty-consciousness, even when money comes to you, you'll slip right back into the place where there doesn't seem to be enough. You'll begin to cling to it and start the cycle all over again.*

The answer to fear leaving you is to develop a prosperity-consciousness. It isn't to get money. It's to *accept* money into your life as your right. Then you will have no fear of circulating it out into the world again to multiply.

Take Action:

Take some time to remember things you may have heard as child. Call up the memories that indicated to you some kind of lack existed in your life.

Review your life as it is today. Are you still acting on childhood limitations? Decide which ones are no longer reasonable and make a concentrated effort to replace those old tapes with new ones.

Holding a door open for a couple of minutes will not run your heating or air conditioning bill sky-high. Old frayed clothing is not "good enough to wear around the house." You need to be making an appearance of prosperity at all times. There is no appropriate time to look - or feel - poor!

Is It Selfish?

Many people believe asking for - or deliberately creating - money is selfish. This goes back to old beliefs that money is at the root of all evil. Therefore, money is "bad." *This belief will defeat you!* Let's change the perception ...

Evil can be defined as "unloving behavior," and money is not the root of unloving behavior. *Fear, in the form of greed,* is at the root of unloving behavior where money is concerned. Money is nothing more than a tool.

Secondly, money is not "bad." We were never intended to live with any kind of lack in our lives. If it takes money to live in our society then we're not intended to have any lack of it. In fact - we're intended to have abundance in all areas of our lives. Money is part of our lives. But, we do have to accept that abundance.

The other issue of possible selfishness is in asking only for ourselves. I'll just let you figure this out. Try to come up with anything you could ask for that would not benefit someone else too. I'll bet you can't do it!

Stop right here! Think about that deeply for a moment. This is a very important question. Can you think of a single thing you could ask for that would not benefit someone else in some manner?

Others are always blessed by your prosperity in all areas. Unless, of course, you want 100 million dollars so you can keep it in a sock under your mattress. All blessings radiate out to others. I'd like for you to think about that the next time you start thinking it's selfish to create money for yourself.

Everything you have brings – has brought – or will bring – good to someone else too!

The First Step to Wealth

Before we can begin to bring what we want into our lives, we need to get rid of the things we don't want. This should be the easiest part of the whole process, but that isn't always true. We tend to want to hang on to things in case we run out later. You'll have to get past that inclination - and do it anyway!

The universe abhors a vacuum. Create a space with nothing in it, and the universe will rush in to fill it. This holds true for our feelings as well as for material things.

When you begin to consciously create your own life, there's always a clean-up job to be done. In order to bring in something new, the old things have to be removed. You will need to create that vacuum.

Banish what you don't want in the same way you banish feelings from old memories. If it's there taking up space - and you don't want it - you are paying some attention to it. You have to let it go!

Occasionally a negative situation turns up you don't want in your life. Giving it attention will cause it to expand. This is when you remove your attention - turning it to something positive. Or, you may find something positive in the situation itself - and focus on that.

Trying to get rid of a situation you don't want is negative attachment. It is still receiving attention and will remain. The energy is still there. What you do not want will fade away when you refuse to give it attention. Remove it from your thinking. Then, relax - and let it go.

Creating a Void

A void is a space with nothing in it. It's the vacuum the universe will rush in to fill. Nature will always attempt to fill a void. If you dig a hole in the ground but don't fill it back up - nature will take care of it for you. The hole will eventually refill itself with more soil, debris or water.

The same thing holds true right in your very home. Let's assume you need a new coffee pot. The old one is limping along - just barely working. But, you keep fooling with it - maybe even cussing it. Giving it negative attention.

Get rid of it! I promise you - even if you think you can't possibly find $30 to buy a new coffee pot - you will find it. That coffee pot will be replaced one way or another!

Maybe you would like to have a new wardrobe. You probably have a closet full of old things - or things that no longer fit. You're keeping them "just in case ..." Give them away! (Give what you wish to receive.) Get those clothes out of your sight. As long as they are hanging in that closet, they have your attention. You see them every time you open the closet door, whether you think about them or not.

Exactly like the coffee pot. Every time you fussed with using it, it was getting attention. We fail to manifest new things as long as we are paying attention to the old stuff. We'll pay attention to the old stuff as long as it's taking up space in our environment.

I once had a student bring up a good point on empty space. He said, "You know - my bank account is darn near empty all the time. Why doesn't the universe rush in to fill *that* void?"

Excellent question. The answer was in the question itself. The attention given to the bank account as empty created even more "empty." What we give our attention to - increases. In this case the attention was on the emptiness of the bank account. So the emptiness increased.

We are actually dealing with what seem like two different issues here - yet they are connected. The first issue is the matter of what you have taking up space. The universe can't fill what's already full. The second issue is what is being increased due to the attention it's given.

Here's why they are connected:

You may have tons of material things laying around you don't want and don't need. You may also be so used to those things, you don't really "see" them anymore. You may think that means you're not giving them attention.

Not true. At the unconscious level you are very aware of these things. They have your attention every time you walk around them. Remember: *if our creative energy isn't deliberately directed from our conscious mind - it will create automatically from the unconscious mind.* The unconscious mind is always paying attention to what's around you.

When the conscious mind begins complaining about something you don't want - the attention becomes negative attachment. You are holding on to it with your complaining. This is why it's so important to control our thoughts. If you don't want it - let it go!

One of the universal laws to always keep in mind when discarding material things:

What you give comes back to you, many times multiplied!

Give what you want to receive. You may have things you no longer care to keep. You want them replaced with something better. Yet, someone else would be delighted to have what you are about to discard. So, don't throw it out. Give it away. This allows the universe to send it back to you in new form. Multiplied. Better - not "more of the same."

If you want love - give love. If you want money - give money. If you want wellness - help someone else be well. These decisions take a bit of thought in order to know exactly what to give. Making those decisions correctly is discussed in Part Three.

You may already have some idea of what material things you would like to bring into your life. Don't get in a hurry. In Part Three, you will learn exactly how to make the right choices for yourself.

Take Action:

Spend this month cleaning up and cleaning out. Review the paragraphs on Feng Shui in the chapter entitled, "Getting Started." I'm not asking you to embrace the Feng Shui philosophy if you're not comfortable with it. However, the basic premises of Feng Shui are universally sound and scientifically correct.

Specifically, I mean the ideas of having "clean" energy around you. Remember that ch'i is the life force energy in the Oriental discipline of Feng Shui. It's just another name for the life force I refer to as "Prana" in the relaxation chapter of the Appendix. Different cultures have different names for this life force energy - but it's all the same. Don't make the mistake of getting bogged down in semantics.

Do everything you can to clean up your environment - all of your different environments. Include every place where you spend your time. Bring in those things that will breathe life into your space. Well-tended plants - fish - circulating water - and especially light. Clean those windows!

Okay - get the maintenance people to clean them. But, get them clean so they can conduct energy in the most efficient manner.

Maybe you don't like your home or office. If that's the case, you have formed a negative attachment. If you want it to increase into a better place, you'd better learn to love it. Do everything you can to give it positive energy.

Take Action:

Look around you carefully to see what's taking up space. Unless it has very positive sentimental value, if you haven't used it in the past year - get rid of it. Give it away.

Look closely at everything. Is it chipped, cracked or torn? Is it too large or too small? Does it look pathetic even after its cleaned? Better an empty space than bedraggled surroundings. Do you really need that Psych 101 textbook from 20 years ago? Are you really ever going to cut the recipes out of those piles of magazines? When is the last time you played tennis with that old frayed racket?

Take Action:

As you are working on getting your physical surroundings cleared and peaceful, begin a daily period of the simple meditation exercise described in the Appendix. Start with 5 minutes a day if that's all you can do comfortably. Here you are clearing your physical body of negative energies - as well as your mind. Don't skip this action technique!

Take Action:

Once your surroundings and your mind are more peaceful, start working on throwing out those old negative belief systems. Take some quiet time to review all of your erroneous beliefs regarding poverty. Pay particular attention to any beliefs you may have concerning your worthiness to have riches. Do this action technique casually for now. We will go into more detail on replacing these beliefs later in The MASTER COURSE.

Physical Well-Being

Our physical well-being is completely our own responsibility. As mentioned in Part One, much of it is based on what we hear, believe and accept for ourselves. I hope by now you have spent some time "listening" to your own words, thoughts and fears.

Fear is the biggest killer of all time. I realize many would say that stress is the biggest killer. But, what is behind stress? Fear. Even eustress - or stress from happy situations - has a certain amount of fear behind it.

Many "alternative" remedies are fast gaining credibility even with the medical profession. Some of these remedies are sometimes considered "New Age." Let me take a moment right here to make something very clear for you.

There's nothing "new" about anything that is today termed "New Age!"
Nothing!

New Age ideas go back to antiquity. As do so-called "New Age" remedies. And, they work. Not that today's artificial remedies dispensed by the medical profession don't work. They work too. But, they all too often have unpleasant - or even unfortunate - side-effects due to the artificial nature of the remedy.

The bottom line is: whatever you can believe in - with all your heart - will work for you. It is, as always, your choice. But there comes a point where you are safer depending on yourself and more natural remedies than on other people's decisions for you.

Would you rather place your trust in yourself and your own positive relationship with your body - or would you rather trust another person standing over you, scalpel in hand? Would you rather keep yourself in top physical condition - or would you rather deal with a bureaucratic insurance company when something goes wrong and they don't want to pay the bill for the treatment you need? The decisions of insurance companies are right behind fear for being killers.

Certain other procedures have been frowned upon by many medical professionals, which are absolutely beneficial to your health - as well as necessary to your energy fields. Your energy field has so much to do with what you create - and how well you create it.

Manipulation of the spinal column is one of these positive procedures. Your most powerful personal energies run along the spinal column. The energies need to run straight and without interference in order to release their greatest power. Therefore, your spinal column needs to stay in place. This is accomplished with infinitely less trauma to the body through manipulation, rather than through surgery.

Many would point out we now live longer than ever and it's because we have better medical technology. Well, yes - and no. Number one - if we are to believe some of the writings of ancient times, we once lived may hundreds of years. Whether you believe that or not is up to you.

We might also take a look at the quality of this so-called longer life span we now have. In many countries, things have changed drastically over the past couple of generations.

Where once our elders were a cherished - and active - part of the family right up until the day they took their final leave, now they are shuffled off to long-term care facilities. There they may lead lives full of loneliness along with feelings of abandonment and worthlessness. Those feelings are nearly always present before the illness or debilitating condition that takes them to "the home."

This is often excused by the insistence they can be better cared for in a facility for that purpose. Unless it is a true hospital facility, this is an excuse! It's a modern changing view on the value of life and the contributions of the elderly. It is also part of the generational mind-sets of, "Me, first!"

This still isn't done in most societies on our planet. In some cultures, the number of years you have lived gains you greater and greater respect. You are honored for your experience and wisdom. You are given back the care, which you gave at an earlier time - without any resentment. Imagine that!

People sometimes tell me they can't take care of the aging parent who gave them life, because they have "responsibilities." I always wonder how they would have felt if that same parent had delivered them to an orphanage when they couldn't take care of themselves as a child. It is true the best way to avoid responsibility is to say, "I've got responsibilities."

These people may need to be reminded: "What goes around, comes around." One day they may be given the opportunity to experience the heartache that goes along with being "kicked to the curb" by the very people they have nurtured over the years. The elderly are seldom any more difficult than their children were for the first 18 years (or more) of their lives.

Obviously, the best thing any of us can do to avoid such situations is to stay well and active in the first place. This does require an ongoing positive relationship with your body. It's never too late. You can choose to develop this relationship at any time you choose.

If fear is the killer - love gives life. Always.

Cell Relationships

Now, our lessons and action techniques will be directed toward developing this positive relationship with your body. Learning to love your body - exactly the way it is today. Not when you lose 30 pounds - not if only those wrinkles weren't there - not if only something were different. Exactly the way it is today. Unconditional love!

> *A positive, loving relationship with every cell in your body must be established if you are to work effectively with your body.*

Begin to think of the cells of your body as your own huge group of supporters. They do support every moment of your life. They never work against you. If you are carrying an extra 30 pounds, this is a signal from your cells that something is amiss. Something needs to be changed. It's merely your cells' way of communicating with you.

The first indication of physical distress is a message from our bodies that something is interfering with their ability to work at peak levels - always stress of one kind or another. The cells' capacity to work for us properly is severely limited by fear energy. If we learn to pay attention to those first signals and remove the fear energy, many ailments would never expand into full-blown dis-eases.

If you are beginning - or well into - the physical signs of age, that is nothing more than your cells demonstrating what you have told them to demonstrate. Your belief in aging signals them to give you what you ask for. It's also true some people just don't care, and that's okay, too.

I'm going to give you two action techniques to practice for one month. You will do one of them at the beginning of your day - the other at the end. Be very consistent in using each of these techniques.

I am guiding you to arrive at a place where you will be able to create your own perfect physical conditions. It must be done in stages. You will not do it overnight. You have had many years of creating your current condition. Now, you may have to reverse that work. Some of the health techniques might feel a bit odd to you. Just do them. You'll become quite comfortable as you establish that positive relationship with your cells.

Take Action:

You will need a full-length mirror. If you don't have one in a private place, find an inexpensive full-length door mirror and hang it on the inside of your bathroom door. This exercise is more difficult for some people than others. You may have avoided looking at your body closely for a long time but now you are about to get acquainted with your life giving support system.

As you begin your day, give yourself a few extra minutes before your shower or bath. Take off all your clothes and stand in front of the mirror. Do not concern yourself with what you believe is wrong with your body. Don't give it any attention.

Look at the image of you in that mirror until you can find something to love about it. No matter how long it takes at first. Don't leave the house until you do it! Find something you appreciate. Now, mentally thank the cells of your body for creating that perfect aspect of you.

Think of it as a rule. The rule is that you cannot continue your day until you find something about your physical body to love.

Then as you proceed to bathe, treat your body with all the kindness you can think of to give it. Relax – use soaps you love – be comfortable – don't hurry. Give your body your full attention. Leave thinking about what you have ahead of you during the day for later.

As you are cleansing your body, concentrate on the idea you are washing away all the negative energies that may have accumulated in your cells during the past 24 hours. Feel them rinse away and go right down the drain.

Start your day refreshed – with all negativity gone – and in love with at least one part of your body.

Take Action:

This technique is to be done at the end of your day as you prepare to sleep. Do it at the time when you settle down, ready to close your eyes. If this is a time when you usually get a lot of "mind chatter" going on - this technique will eliminate that.

Mentally picture yourself in front of the mirror you used earlier in the day. Again, sans clothing. Nothing may be pictured here except your body itself.

Now, see in your mind exactly the image you would like to see in that mirror. All of this will be done only in your mind. Make it a very vivid picture. Know this is your image you are looking at!

You do not get to picture the person you most admire physically in that mirror! You must make the picture your perfect image of your own body. Whatever that is.

At first, create yourself! Design your body! Be realistic. After you've done this a few times, you'll arrive at the image you truly want to see when you look in the real mirror. Now, you will want to lock in this image of yourself.

Remember, your cells "hear" your thoughts and "see" what is pictured in your mind. Although they do have intelligence, they cannot tell the difference between what is in the outer world - and what is in your inner thought world. They will accept your mental images as true. They will then move to bring about the conditions imaged in your mind.

Eventually, you may have to do something in the outer to help them with their creation. But, it won't be difficult. If you are seeing yourself 30 pounds lighter, you will soon begin to lose your appetite for additional or fattening foods. It is quite unlike dieting. You may not even notice your eating habits changing at first. The cells have simply begun sending you different signals.

Or, maybe you're seeing yourself as very muscular and physically fit - yet you hate to exercise. If you do this mental exercise consistently, you may very well find you suddenly develop an interest and enthusiasm for the gym. But again, it will be quite different from forcing yourself to work out.

Very often, however, I've noticed absolutely nothing is changed in the outer. Yet, the imaged changes will manifest anyway. Quite unexplainable. Also, quite true.

Take Action:

This is a very simple one. Begin now to think of a name for the cells of your body. Soon, you will begin addressing the cells of your body directly when you give them instructions.

You need to establish a very personal relationship with the cells of your body. Since there are so many of them, it's easier to address them as group. Remember, these cells support your life and literally respond to your direction.

I have no idea why, but I personally address the cells of my own body as "Guys." It has nothing to do with gender. When I "speak" to them it's very personal. For instance, upon entering a city full of smog, I think to my cells, "Okay Guys, we need to ignore all the filth in the air while we're here." And, they do! I will experience no physical response to anything in that air.

Out of some sort of habit, we tend to treat our bodies as if they aren't a part of us. As if they are the enemy trying to defeat us. In truth, we are our own worst enemies when it comes to our physical condition. And, it isn't so much what we do to our bodies as it is our failure to take charge and lead the troops.

Decide right now - you are 100% in charge of your body and you have a devoted army of cells waiting for your orders. Appreciate them - and give them direction!

Herbs & Vitamins

Our bodies appreciate and respond to natural remedies from other living cells. It isn't a good idea to introduce synthetic drugs into the body unless absolutely necessary. Many unenlightened medical professionals continue to deny the value of herbal remedies, mostly due to ignorance of their actual value to the human immune system.

A very few years ago, pharmaceutical companies were busy denying the effectiveness of herbal remedies for physical distress. This is no longer the case as they are now selling the very products they disparaged.

No matter which way this issue swings, natural remedies will always be of the utmost value to physical well-being. *Life responds to life.* Herbal remedies come directly from life.

It is true our modern civilization with all its technological advances is ruining our environment and making it more difficult to sustain life. We once received the herbs and vitamins that strengthen our cells through natural means. Today, we need to replace vitamins, which are drained from our bodies and ingest herbs in more deliberate ways. You won't find many herbs in the cooking done by the microwavable food producers. The natural vitamins in food are being destroyed by our modern preservation and cooking processes.

I will not attempt to advise you on which herbs and vitamins you need to take. That is an individual thing determined by the cells of your own body. Our bodies tell us what they need by the signals they send.

Determine what seems to be a little "off." Then find a reputable, natural herb and vitamin shop and get some help. Read labels. Do not load up on everything in the store. Only choose those products recommended for your particular problem. Many good books on this subject are available. Try to find one that is not slanted toward selling the writer's own products.

Always buy only natural products. Don't bother with the synthetics. You might as well chew gum for all the good they will do. Remember, you are looking for life to sustain life. Synthetics aren't made from living cells. Herbal teas are one of the most effective methods of taking natural herbs.

Also, please don't try to double up on the recommended dosages. More is not better - or faster. In fact, more could be harmful. Give yourself at least 90 days to see if the particular product you bought will make a difference. If not, do try another.

Aroma Therapy

(Men! Do not skip this chapter!)

Never doubt that aromas can give very real therapeutic results. Scent has amazing restorative power. However, as with many "therapies," some practitioners are inclined to make it much more complicated than is necessary. This can become especially problematic when directed toward some men who may not be able to generate much enthusiasm for sitting around smelling the flowers.

So, Gentlemen, before we go any further with this - how do you feel about the smell of fresh-cut grass - or a smoldering hickory log - or sizzling garlic toast - or pine needles?

You see? Many different types of scents exist in this world - not just herbs and flowers. The whole idea of aroma therapy is to shift - or create - moods. It's why both men and women wear colognes or perfumes.

A familiar scent is the quickest way to bring up a memory. Our sense of smell is the most closely connected to our emotions. It also has a direct link to the part of the brain that controls our feelings and moods. When you notice an aroma that reminds you of a happy time in your past, the positive, happy feelings of love kick into gear instantly.

I'm not suggesting you should live in the past. I'm suggesting it is always to your benefit to invoke happy feelings and surround yourself in those energies. Feelings create. When we want to create positive circumstances - we need to keep ourselves surrounded with the most positive, happy feelings.

You can buy a multitude of books, which will instruct you as to which scents are supposed to accomplish which results. But the bottom line is which scents accomplish the desired results for you. For instance, the scent of lavender - which is highly touted for relaxation - will do nothing but irritate me. I don't like it - so how could it ever induce relaxation for me? It can't.

As with everything else - this is a very personal area that should always be specific to what you require. Aroma therapy is to be used to help you create the moods - therefore the emotions - which will help you create your desires. Scents that please you reduce stress and create positive energies around you.

You can find a myriad of ways to bring the scents that please you into your space. Of course, you can use the obvious things, i.e., candles - scented plants - potpourri pots. But, you can also find other ways. For instance, you could put scented candles in an electric potpourri pot - and put it out of sight. The candle wax will slowly melt and fill your space with scent - all without any visible evidence of the scent in sight. (Just don't forget to turn it off when you leave the room!)

Essential oils are widely available and come in a multitude of scents. Flower fragrances, of course, but also citrus, fruity, woody, and minty. A few drops of essential oil with a bit of water in a lamp ring, set atop a light bulb, will last for hours and infuse a room with your favorite aroma. Or, use your imagination and find a way to bring your very favorite scent into your space.

Be sure to look for a shop or source that carries a large choice of scents. You might also like to mix your own. I personally like a 50-50 mix of light musk and vanilla.

One word of caution: Chemical reproductions of essential oils do not work. You need the true essential oil for best results. Due to the strong concentration of the essence of the plants used, just a very few drops will give the needed results. Essential oils, however, should not be applied to the skin full-strength - and should never be taken internally without a thorough education in their use.

In Part Three of *The MASTER COURSE*, we will go into quite a bit more depth on the subject of stress and how it affects health, youth and physical well-being. We will begin more action techniques aimed to reduce stress and replace it with the feelings of peace needed to create all life transformations.

> *Nothing in The MASTER COURSE life transformation Course is intended to take the place of professional medical treatment. If you have a serious medical condition, please see a medical professional. The ideas in this Course are intended to prevent, rather than treat, illness or debilitating conditions.*

Intimate Relationships

Before we jump into creating lasting relationships, we need to do the head work. The heart work comes later. We also need to expand on a subject from Part One - the subject of loving yourself first.

You may have spent many years criticizing yourself - judging yourself - carrying your self-esteem down around your ankles. If you wish to have a truly loving and balanced relationship, this has to stop! Otherwise, you'll only attract those who are more than happy to help you sustain this low opinion of yourself.

Remember, every thought you have creates an energy field around you. It's the energies in this field that go out to attract others who are carrying the complementary energies.

To be more specific, let's say you believe you are somehow unworthy and deserve to be treated poorly. The complementary energy is in someone who has a need to treat another person poorly. You come into contact with this person with complementary energy and – Bingo! You are each instantly attracted to the other. It's a magnetic attraction.

This may all be at the unconscious level. You may not have a clue you actually feel that way about yourself. This is especially - and extremely - important for anyone who has ever been involved in an abusive relationship - of any kind.

And yes - women can be abusive just as easily as men. Men don't have any corner on abuse. There are many kinds of abuse. It may be physical - mental - or emotional. Anyone can be abusive and sadly, many don't even realize they are being so.

Here's the test for unfulfilling relationships:

Take Action:

Look at your past relationships - the ones that brought sorrow rather than joy. Is there some kind of sameness about the type of people you were with? It may have manifested in different ways - but it would be there. Sit down and make a list. Think about those relationships carefully. Find the similarities.

Then, think carefully about what energies you might be projecting to attract this type of person. Again - make a list. Write down every unkind thought you ever had about yourself. See if there is a pattern there inviting certain types of behavior from others.

If you have been involved in past unhappy relationships, it's very important you use the above technique. If you wish to create a lasting and fulfilling relationship, you will need to change your energy patterns. You can't change something until you are aware of it.

Your next step will be to create positive energies regarding who you are and what you deserve to have in life. In order to do this, you will need to find - and change every negative thing you believe about yourself.

Sometimes, negative thoughts and images about the self are merely a matter of some bad habits. If this is the case, it's usually a simple matter to stop your negative thoughts simply by paying attention and stopping them when they come up. You would immediately replace the thought with something you consider very positive about yourself.

I also understand this can be a project all by itself if the problem is serious. You'll find help for this in *The MASTER COURSE* Workbook.

The bottom line is, *you must create positive energies in your energy field* if you hope to attract someone who will have those same - and complementary - energies. Without that, you can use all the techniques for creating your desired fulfilling relationship for years - yet continue to attract exactly what you do not want!

It's an absolute truth:
the more you work on you - the less you'll have to work on others!

Infatuation vs. Love

Next, we need to define "love," since I assume you would like to have a loving relationship. I've always loved Gertrude Stein's definition. She simply said, "Love is."

Too often we confuse "love" with infatuation. There's a big difference. Infatuation can happen almost instantly. Love takes a while. On the next page is a definition of the two, which may help you to sort out your feelings at any given time.

Infatuation Is:
Knots in the pit of your stomach
Utter despair when the phone doesn't ring
Imagined slights - Nightmares
Electricity at the barest touch
Dread of an empty tomorrow
Killing time until the next meeting
Ignoring faults -
by pretending they don't exist
A wrenching and constant heartache
Frantic - Grasping - Destructive
And quite common
A state of mind which cannot endure

Infatuation hurts
And dies.

Love Is:
Holding hands on a rainy day
Laughter for absolutely no reason
Sharing rainbows and daydreams
Warmth in a circle of arms
Having faith in each tomorrow
Feeling every moment of life
Recognizing human limitations -
and accepting them
A peaceful and quiet happiness
Calm - Giving - Creative
And often rare
A state of heart which always endures

Love heals
And lives.

Infatuation - is a lonely thing
Love - is for two.

You may have noticed the extreme reactions in infatuation. It is extreme. It feels powerful. Yet, it won't make it over the long haul. Where love is involved, we may be excited about seeing the one we truly love - but we won't be in turmoil over it. We may miss them when they aren't available to us - but we won't completely shut down and curl up in a dark corner until they return.

We need to have patience at the beginning of any intimate relationship. Take it slow. Too often, when the hormones turn on - the brain turns off.

Many people believe we should just let love happen - that we shouldn't have preconceived ideas. It's true - love doesn't come with instructions - and most of us would never read them if it did. But, then we're going in brain-dead. It's best to do the thinking before it happens. Work out the issues before they come up.

Take Action:

Take some time to think what love really means to you. How do you want to feel within a relationship? Picture yourself with the partner you would like to have. What are you doing? What do you share? How do you feel when this person isn't around? Begin now to create the picture of the relationship you wish to create. Not the person you want - the relationship itself.

Deciding What It Takes

Nearly everyone would like to have a relationship with their partner close to the kind of relationship we have with a best friend. At least we would like for the relationship to be similar. With a true best friend we have utter safety and total validation within the relationship. To enter into an intimate relationship with someone with whom you can't be friends is self-defeating. Every time!

Take Action:

Write out your picture of being in a relationship where you do have utter safety and total validation. Exactly what does this mean to you? Exactly what would you need to receive from another person to feel this way? Be realistic. Never expect to receive from another what you are not willing to give!

Do not throw this list away. Keep it to refer to in the future. You may also find it takes you awhile to write a complete list.

In order for a relationship to last, both people need to be whole and complete within themselves. Then, neither is taking from the other in an effort to get something perceived to be missing within the self. We know who we are - we know who they are - and it's okay! Then we can join together to form an even larger whole.

Nobody else can ever make us happy. That's an inside job. We must be reasonably happy before we will attract a lasting relationship. However, we can simply know what it takes to be happy within a relationship.

Be very honest about this. Get the answers set firmly in your head. In the beginning of a relationship, we are so enthralled with the good feelings we tend to overlook important things. Yet, this is the very time when we most need to be paying attention to the characteristics of the possible partner. You don't want to accept something in the beginning that will make you angry, or unhappy, later.

Personality Characteristics

You should be aware that certain personality characteristics are probably inborn. It can be nearly impossible to get another person to change behavior stemming from these innate traits.

You may believe the person who is late all the time is an inconsiderate boor. In fact, some people are carelessly - or even deliberately - late, as a way of discounting another's importance.

On the other hand, this person may actually perceive time in a different way than you do. This same person may be quite spontaneous and able to make or change plans easily, whereas, you may like to plan ahead and schedule your activities. Believe me when I tell you - you will need to accept this difference or find another choice of partner.

Introverts and extroverts can learn to live with each other's traits. You might even get the introvert to go out more - but you'll never make them like it. And, you will never turn them into the life of the party. Nor, can you ever expect the extrovert to be happy sitting home reading books all the time.

You have two other areas that can make understanding between two people difficult. One person may take in information through the five physical senses, and the other may gather information intuitively. The sensing person has some difficulty understanding why the intuitive person can't remember details.

The intuitive can't remember the details because she never took them in to begin with. The intuitive gets the big picture and could tell you all the moods and feelings involved in a situation - but never noticed what anyone was wearing.

The fourth personality trait needing to be understood is how people make decisions. Some people prefer to make decisions by thinking through all the facts. Others make decisions based on their feelings about the situation. This one is extremely difficult to understand when you are interacting with someone who has the trait opposite to yours.

It's asking too much to expect another to go against their inborn personality traits. I'm assuming here you would like for your partner to be as happy in the relationship as you would like to be. This is an area where great understanding and acceptance is in order.

You can pick up a copy of *"Please Understand Me: Character & Temperament Types"* by David Kersey and Marilyn Bates, in nearly any library. It contains a shorter version of a similar inventory questionnaire used by psychological counselors.

This book will allow you to find out your own personality preferences - as well as help you understand them in others. It will also help you understand how the different types can interact with each other most constructively and with the least amount of tension. When we understand why someone acts - or reacts - in the way they do, it's much easier to avoid taking it personally.

Expectations

WRITE this down somewhere: *The level of your frustration is directly proportional to the level of your expectations.* Unreasonable expectations will bring you nothing but frustration. Reasonable expectations are another matter.

You may have heard it is unfair to have expectations in a relationship. Not true! A relationship is a type of contract. We do have expectations of what should happen within that relationship whether we admit them or not. In fact - we must have certain expectations in regard to our rights within the partnership. You have an absolute right within a relationship:

- To be treated with dignity and respect

- To have your feelings honored

- Not to be around crazy behavior

- Not to be abused in any way - whether physical, emotional or mental

- Not to be lied to, manipulated or coerced

You can only expect these things, however, if you have communicated your expectations. How to do that? Speak up! It is okay to talk about it early on in the relationship. In fact, it's imperative to talk about it as soon as possible.

You will have to be willing to communicate what "having your feelings respected" means to you. Not everyone would define "dignity and respect" in the same way. These are not subjects to leave to guesswork! You may not expect someone to read your mind - unless, of course, you would like to have them read it incorrectly.

What we have no right to expect in a relationship is to have the other person make us happy. We can give enjoyment within a relationship but we cannot make someone happy.

When you enter into a partnership you are making an agreement to be together. It's completely wrong to assume you can do that effectively without each knowing what the other expects. It is a type of contract.

I know it doesn't sound very romantic. It may sound too businesslike to appeal to you. If so - it's time for another change of perception. Your life within a relationship is your business! Failed relationships aren't terribly romantic either.

Take Action:

Review your lists from "Deciding What it Takes." These are the things you will need to communicate to a potential relationship partner. Now expand the answers to those lists to begin being more specific about how you recognize those needs being met.

I learned quite a lot about relationships in a book entitled, *"Stage II Relationships"* by Earnie Larsen. It's a book written for people recovering from addiction. However, it works for all people who wish to form good, stable, intimate relationships. Having gone through a few unfortunate relationships myself, I found the missing keys in this valuable book! I highly recommend it!

Doing the Groundwork

THE first two Parts of *The MASTER COURSE* are directed to specifically laying groundwork for the creative processes taught later in this Course. You may wonder, "When do we get to the actual creation of life transformation?"

Rest assured - we'll get there!

When new students come to me telling me they have tried dozens of creative techniques, but nothing lasts - I know exactly what has happened. They never did the groundwork. Nor, did they ever develop the mind-sets that will make their creations last.

They have read some excellent books and tried to jump right into using the techniques taught there. This can't be done if you expect to bring permanent transformation into your life. You can't build a castle on top of a shack. First, you will have to tear down the shack.

Sometimes, I get the response of, "My God! I have to change everything about myself!" No - not at all.

The things keeping you from having what you want don't belong to you. They are ideas put there by other people. They have nothing to do with who you truly are. What we are tearing down are the positions of other people. We are peeling away layers of false information about who you truly are. We are also uncovering what is right for you!

Please do not become impatient and decide you'll just skip the preparatory material and go straight to the creative processes. These action techniques I'm asking you to do are designed to allow you to begin building a new picture of yourself. They will ultimately allow you to claim your own being. You will soon begin to decide for yourself what makes you happy - rather than what you think *should* make you happy.

If you are serious about creating a life of fulfillment and joy - make some time to work toward that goal every day. Do the "Take Action" techniques in this book as thoroughly as possible. Read over every chapter until you completely understand what needs to be achieved. Prepare yourself for a whole new - and wonderful - life!

It's very important to pay attention at all times. You will be watching your thoughts and feelings constantly. You will be deliberately replacing any fear thoughts with something positive.

You will need to consciously look around you at the environment where you spend your time. Take note of everything about it. Decide how it makes you feel.

Consider every friend you spend time with – every television show, or movie, you watch – every book you read. Begin to decide what brings fear thoughts into your world. Decide if, and how, you will replace these activities with something positive.

You will be practicing holding good, loving thoughts about yourself in your mind for short periods of time. You will practice rejecting all unloving fear thoughts for yourself during that time period. Gradually lengthen the time.

Please spend plenty of time on the "Take Action" exercises, and do them carefully. Write down everything that comes to your mind as you do them. Some of these ideas will need to be rejected now. If you find you are having any problems with the concepts, go back to Part One for review.

Keep your life transformation right in the front of your mind as much as possible. Allow it to begin affecting everything you do!

Part Three

Introduction to Part Three

THE first two Parts of *The MASTER COURSE* have led you through the "cleaning out" necessary before we can build something new. By now, you should also be getting into the habit of surrounding yourself with the creative life energies within your environment(s).

You may remember from Part One that we often need to learn processes to take control of our lives. From this point on, please remember that processes are only tools. They aren't necessarily something you will need to do for the rest of your life.

You may come back to certain processes if you find yourself slipping in some area. That's okay. Pick up your tools. Bear in mind though that the process itself has no power. A process simply helps you focus. It helps you change habits. That's all.

Never give your power away to a process – or to another person.

What you are actually doing with *The MASTER COURSE* is learning to manipulate energies. The energies are there for our use. We manipulate them all the time without realizing it. Now, we are learning to manipulate energy in such a way that we bring about the most positive results. We use the processes as tools for that purpose.

Once again, please read all chapters of *The MASTER COURSE* even if a particular subject isn't what you feel you need to create right now.

Remember all processes are interchangeable. Something from another chapter may be exactly what you need.

On the subject of power, we have an issue that needs to be addressed before we get too deeply into using the processes. Many people believe we ultimately have no power at all. It can certainly seem that way at times.

Things do happen over which we have no control. Natural disasters are a good example. In truth, every person affected by a natural disaster had some fear of loss going on before the disaster hit. If they hadn't, they would have been away at the time - or they would have been living in another location, altogether. On the other side of that coin, sometimes very good things come out of "disasters." The rough times will pass and we may be left with something better.

We also have little control over the lives of others. The lives of other people can affect us dramatically. Even as I write this, my life is being affected by a mistake made by another person. I have two choices in the matter.

I could let the energy of fear take over and become upset. I could jump right in and start trying to "fix" it. I could tell everyone about it, thereby allowing my words to become the vehicle for carrying that fear energy out into the universe where it will only make the situation worse.

Or, I can hold to the absolute good of life and know it will be resolved with a minimum of chaos. I can step back and realize this isn't my lesson, but I am only being affected by the lesson of another. I can also send positive energy to the person who is actually responsible for correcting the situation.

After the circumstances pass, I can look at the situation and decide what I can do to keep such a thing from affecting me again. At that point, I won't be doing anything out of desperation. Therefore, fear energy will not be directing my decisions.

All fear is the result of perceived loss - whether it loss of our money - our loved ones - or our health. It's either fear we won't get something we want - or fear we will lose something we have.

Change of perception: We have very little that couldn't be replaced with something better. When something is taken from us - or leaves our life - this is the most important time to change our perception. Rather than allowing it to throw us completely off center - we can remain open to the possibilities of something better. We must accept something better before it can come to us.

Where loved ones are concerned - *love can never be taken away from us.* What we experienced with them before they left will be there forever.

Universal Laws

Now it's time to take a look at the universal *laws* that the universal *principles* are driving. You can find a myriad of supposed universal laws. However, for our purposes, we'll just address the main ones that help us create our lives.

We aren't talking about physical laws or scientific laws here - although those laws also change as we learn more. For instance, the law of gravity would seem to be absolute - yet, it isn't. The law of gravity has been defied.

The universal laws we're concerned with are spiritual laws. They are always there - they always work. But, it's the principles taught in Part One that decide how the law works. These are the universal laws we are always using in creating our own lives. How they will work in your transformation process is determined by whether you can accept and embrace the universal principles in Part One.

Law of Love

St. Francis of Assisi said this best. *"It is in giving love that we receive love."*

If we try to love as unconditionally as possible, we will always receive love back. When we withhold love, we may eventually find ourselves loveless. This is the law that works to keep our love when we put our relationships first - over the ego's need to be "right."

Law of Forgiveness

To be forgiven you must forgive. Forgiveness is a cleansing process so, of course, it is something we will try to do before creating more happiness for our lives. Nearly everyone also has things they need to be forgiven for! How can we expect to be forgiven if we're not willing to forgive?

As with the law of love - it is in forgiving others that we forgive ourselves. We cannot be forgiven until we first forgive others.

Law of Attraction

I know you've heard that opposites attract, but with spiritual law - like attracts like. Even when it seems opposite!

For instance, you may think you are in a relationship with someone who is your total opposite. Not true. When the two of you were attracted to each other, it was because each of you was putting out energies that would fit together to bring about a result you each expected, although it may have been at the unconscious level. Like attracts like.

Law of Abundance

As a person feels in their heart - so are they. You may have heard that statement as "As a person thinks in their heart - so are they." The "heart" part is correct but, of course, we don't think with our hearts! By now, you should already have begun to understand it is the feelings behind a thought that create - not the thought itself.

This law rules the fact that what we hold in our consciousness expresses as situations in our lives. It is the unconscious ruling our beliefs and feelings. The unconscious is the "feeling mind." Bringing those feelings into the conscious mind allows us to change them - and create abundance from full consciousness.

Law of Cause and Effect

Sometimes called the "law of mind action." Every effect has a cause. Every outcome is the result of some action. Change the cause and you change the effect - or - change the action and you change the outcome. This is also the law that brings about the statement, "Chaos comes before order." Sometimes, chaos is necessary before order can be restored.

Law of Empowerment

This is basically the law governing our free will. We have free will to action. But, we also have free will to choose our thoughts - and change our feelings. This gives us total power to keep our attention on the goal. In fact, our attention is always on some aspect of reaching our goals. Too often, it's on the fear that we won't make it!

We have full power to remove our attention from the things we do not want. Then, we can refocus on the positive outcomes we wish to create.

Law of Karma

For every action there is a reaction - or consequence. It can be either harmonious or disharmonious. Nearly all of the other laws could be placed under the law of karma. Karma is dealt with in our lives right now - every day!

What goes out must come back. When we give good - we receive good in return. When we give disharmony - we receive disharmony in return. In other words, we truly do, "reap what we sow."

Everything works both ways!

If you attend to these laws carefully, you'll see everything works both ways! This is the whole point of using the universal *principles* correctly. As long as you understand and accept the universal principles in Part One, the laws will always work for you in the most positive manner. You will always arrive at the correct answer, i.e., 2 + 2 will always equal 4. You'll never get the disharmonious answer of 5.

Start at the Beginning

"Where do I start?"

This is a question I hear often from people who wish to transform any part of their lives. First of all, be assured you have already started. The fact you are reading this Course is evidence of that. *Your entire life is a "work in progress."* With the proper perspective, life just gets better and better. Start with your perspective. Keep it positive! If it isn't positive - change it! We've already covered that.

Next – Call on your power of *movement*!

Decide what you want. What you really, truly want! Those answers are within you. How to you move yourself forward? What makes you feel free and full of energy? What makes life worth living for you? What makes you want to get started in the morning?

Now, what makes you want to lie in a corner in the fetal position? And, what drags you down and makes you struggle to get through your day?

Start doing the things that make you feel happy and alive! Start doing the things that give you power and make you glad to start each day. And, stop doing those things that cause you to dread each new day. Where is it written you should drag through life doing things that stunt your growth?

You feel it in your gut. The things that drag you down were likely taught to you by other people. You may have been taught what is "right" to do.

You may have also been taught that you should feel good about it. Yet, it may not feel good to you at all. Then of course, you may have those little guilt pangs because you don't feel the way you "should." Yikes!

Now, you feel even worse! Are you beginning to see where you need to change your perceptions? You may even need to adjust your ideas about what is right and wrong. Begin with - who said so? And, why?

Never forget you are a unique individual. No - you are not "exactly like your father." Or, your mother.

Imagine you buy some land to build a new home. The land is covered in weeds and in the middle is a little shack. Do you want to live in that shack? Probably not. You'll most likely tear down the shack, mow all the weeds and build your new home on the land they once occupied.

This is where you start. Ask yourself the questions. Weeds and old junk standing in our way is obvious. The things draining your life of happiness may not be so obvious. Or - you may be denying their existence. But - you know! You start by deciding what to throw out. What ideas need to go?

Here's an example. A rather silly example but it will show you just how easy it is to continue to do things based on the ideas of others.

A few years ago, someone asked me why I never wore jeans. Not only didn't I wear jeans - I didn't even own a pair of jeans. I answered automatically, "Girls don't wear jeans!" The second I heard that come out of my mouth, I realized I was channeling my mother. Those were her words!

I was 40 years old. I had three teen-age daughters - all of whom I allowed to wear jeans. And yet, I was still operating *for myself* by what my mother had taught me as a child, when I wanted to dress like my brothers! How silly is that? And, how free do you think I felt when I bought, and started wearing, jeans?

Take Action:

Spend some time thinking about all the things you'd like to do / have / be. Then, think about what's stopping you. Go deep within and try to remember if you've been told some reason you can't – or shouldn't – do that. Write it all down!

For now – just get it on paper where you can see it. You will be referring to this in the next action technique.

Take Action:

Go back over the list you just made – one point at a time. If you find you are doing – or not doing – something because you have embraced the ideas of others, think carefully.

Think for yourself! Are those reasons valid? Do they apply to your life?

In any area where you find they do not – make another decision. What is right for you? What are you going to change? Write it down. Then, do it!

Getting What You Want

THREE main areas of life determine our overall contentment. Those areas are: financial security - relationships of all types - health and physical well-being. In fact, all life challenges fit into one of these three categories.

The unconscious ways in which most people try to accomplish contentment in those areas will vary, dependent upon their core beliefs. Consciously, we may also try using various techniques and processes purposefully to get what we want. I know. I tried them all - until I learned the unchanging principles that bring - not change - but transformation.

Having deliberately done all these things, I tend to see the ridiculous in our human condition when we're trying to get something from some power "out there." Our personal power is always within. Following are examples of some of the things people do to try to bring what they want into their lives.

Some believe in - and rely upon - "luck" or "fate" as the determining factor in whether their life is happy and successful or filled with uncertainty and problems. Their position is, "Nothing we can do about it, so we might as well just live with it."

They feel completely powerless and dependent on the whims of the gods. This is called "resignation" and when life gets very tough, usually turns to self-pity ("Why me?") – then, anger ("Why am I even on this stupid planet?") – and, finally - depression. Help!

Some of these types do try to get help through the use of such things as rites, charms, superstition, or even prayer. They use these processes in an effort to change what they don't believe can be changed in any other possible fashion.

Prayer, by the way, has a much broader definition than is usually thought of by those who use it begging to have wishes granted. Prayer can be a simple, "Thank you." We pray any time we are speaking - or sending thought - directly to the universal spirit.

I know many people (including myself) have been taught nothing happens by mistake - that everything is exactly the way it's supposed to be in any given moment. That's true. Yet, many don't realize whatever is happening is determined by our - often unconscious - expectations and intent.

It is not caused by any power outside ourselves. We only have two positions. We either created it - or we have accepted it as necessary to our learning. And, in either case, we are free to make other choices - and other decisions.

Others believe their own hard work, in all areas, determines their ultimate success. Or, they're sure, if they are just "good enough," they'll be rewarded with the things that will make them happy. By "good enough" I mean doing the "right thing." The "right thing" of course is usually determined by their personal beliefs - and may bear no relation to reality.

Often, those who hold this particular "bargaining" belief are bewildered when the good things don't materialize. After all, their ceaseless efforts to do good - or be good - "should" have brought (or "bought") the good stuff. What's even worse is when they have a number of years of contentment - and then the worm turns - as life becomes just one problem after another.

This is the employee who was on call 24/7 and got all the promotions - but eventually ended up in a cardiac care unit.

It's the one of a couple who bowed to every whim of the other until "the other" went looking for excitement someplace else.

It's also the health enthusiasts who worked out religiously, drank nothing stronger than mineral water, let no fat cross their lips, lobbied for smokers to be put in concentration camps - then, one day was hit by a car and spent the rest of their life snacking on prescription drugs.

Talk about rage! After all they've done? Followed, of course, by depression. Are you beginning to see why depression is so rampant in our society today? We do have a lot of "shoulds."

Now don't get me wrong. I'm not criticizing anyone's efforts to be a good person. A truly loving person, however, acts without any thought of reward. In the cases I cited above, the "good" actions are done in hopes of gaining certain personal benefits. "I'll be good so I'll get good."

And, even that is in line with the universal law that states we receive back what we give. Unfortunately, universal laws are not absolute. Only *principles* are absolute. In order for a law to work every time, we must grasp the principle that lies under the law - and makes it functional. What a person thinks of as being "good" may not be in line with universal principles.

In fact, let's use that law as an example. "What goes out must come back" is the actual law behind receiving back what we give. One of the principles driving that law is, "Spirit is Love."

When we do "good" things because we feel we must do them in order to get back something good, we are actually creating with the fear energy. We fear if we don't do something in a certain way we will pay for it in a negative way. The doing is done out of fear.

When we do these same "good" things out of love - with no expectation of return - we are using the principle correctly. We know life will return the good things. We don't even have to think about it. Fear of not doing them doesn't enter our minds. Now we will create only the good stuff.

Different people would see different scenes in the picture they consider perfect for their particular life. Most dream of a life full of loving relationships - abundant and lasting prosperity - and perfect health. Yet the dream continues to be elusive. At best, our successes are too often transitory - or we do quite well in some area but have continued challenges in others.

In order to experience transformation, all three areas of life must be satisfactory - and stay that way! It's a proven fact it can be done. When this is accomplished, the only "changes" are enhancements to make life even better. The butterfly won't change back to a caterpillar. It will always grow stronger - fly higher.

In truth, there is no reason why everyone can't enjoy financial abundance, satisfying relationships, glowing health - even perpetual youth - and tremendous success in all areas of life. At the same time! It's a simple matter of where you believe the power is.

Ask yourself right now - where is the power that controls your life? If you answer it is within yourself, yet you still aren't living the life of your choice, then ask yourself, "Why?" If the answer to that question is that someone - or something - is standing in your way, then you have the true answer to where you believe the power controlling your life actually is.

For years I've had students, who attend my Transforming Life seminars for the first time, tell me they certainly aren't new to using the creative processes to move their lives in a more positive direction. They learn the techniques - they use the techniques - the techniques work. Then suddenly, everything stops working! More often than not, they even begin to backslide.

Ouch! I've done it myself. And, I can assure you nothing is more discouraging than to know you can bring about change, then have to stand helplessly by while you watch it float away. Possibly leaving you in worse shape than when you started.

So, how do we create transformation, rather than temporary change? The simple answer is: we begin to understand and accept who we are. We realize the power of our expectations and intent. And, we use the underlying principles of creation to express perfection in our human condition.

Yes, we must first dismiss many deeply embedded beliefs, attitudes and judgments from our being. We must empty out the vessel before we can refill it with the truths that create real transformation.

Take Action:

Now is good time to stop and think about why you do some of the things you do to bring good into your life. Choose an area where you do certain things with the idea of creating some circumstance you wish to have in your life. Ask yourself the following questions:

- Am I doing these things because I "should" do them?

- If so, why do I believe that? Is this information really valid for me?

- Would I do these things if I didn't have some expectation of return?

- Do I feel any resentment from the necessity of doing these things?

- How can I accept this good into my life without bargaining for it?

Please continue to work with the idea that we create our lives only through:

- Decision
- Commitment
- Intent
- Acceptance of our good

Making Choices

Rather than running hither and yon through life, we need to make some specific choices. This is especially true when we set out to create specific things for our lives. Believe it, or not, we don't always know what we want. We only have general ideas.

Choices will need to be made no matter which area of life you are attempting to create - or transform. Unconscious choices are always driving our creations. Now, it's time to make them conscious. We'll start with the generalizations that apply to all areas of life. You'll find specifics in the chapters on each subject.

If you have worked through the action techniques in Parts One and Two, you have been examining your past. By now, you should have found some choices that were made for you. It isn't always obvious of course. Your expectations are a direct clue to your choices. Yet, your expectations may have been implanted by others. You have exercised your choice only through your agreement - or acceptance - of the idea.

Think about what you *really* want in your life. Is it health - wealth - loving and happy relationships? All three? I hope so, because - you can have it all.

Next, you will need to examine your desires. For instance, do you think you want to be a millionaire? Well, maybe you do. Or - maybe you just want to be free of financial pressure. This is finding the true basis of the desire you believe you have. The desire may not be what you think it is at all.

Take Action:

Off the top of your head, make a list of everything you would like to have in your life. Be specific.

Look at each item on your list and ask yourself if what you have written is what you truly want. Find the most basic desire involved in your wish. Use the example above.

Is it wealth you want – or is it release from financial pressure? Do you want perpetual youth – or do you just want to feel younger than you perceive yourself to be now? Do you want a long-term committed relationship – or do you simply want to banish loneliness? Get to the bottom of it.

Understand I am not asking you to "settle" for anything. We were never intended to settle for any less than exactly what we want. In fact, settling limits the universe. Settling is a grave mistake. Always set your sights on the most you can have in any area.

We have two things at work here. First, you will only be able to demonstrate in your life what you truly believe you deserve – and what you can accept.

This will increase as time goes on and you become more comfortable with having what you want. In the beginning, you don't want to price yourself right out of business. As you begin to see the manifestation of your desires, your level of what you can accept will rise.

This is why it isn't wise to settle for less than you want over the long-term. The universe will always provide as much as you can accept at any given point in time.

Secondly, we need to examine the age-old adage, "Be careful what you ask for, as you will surely get it." How many times have you asked for something – received it – only to wish later you had never asked? This happens for one reason. We don't stop to consider the ramifications of what we are asking to have.

Take Action:

Go back to the list you made above. Look at each item on your list and ask yourself the following questions. Be extremely honest. Saying, "I'll deal with it when the time comes," is avoiding the issue.

- How will your life change if you manifest exactly what you want? Be very detailed here.

- Are you willing to accept those changes and everything that goes along with them?

- Can you live with it?

- Are you sure you *want* to live with it?

- Are you absolutely sure?

I'd also like to urge you to think very carefully before you try to manifest anything in your life requiring a certain response on the part of a particular person. Don't get your control issues going on this thing. It's very tempting. Believe me - I know! Just go for what is best for your life and leave those other people alone.

The next thing you will need to consider is this: what are you willing to do to help manifest your desire? What are you willing to do to keep that desire once it appears in your life? In other words - what's it worth to you?

We often forget - even using creative energies consciously - there will be things for us to do. We may even need to change things about ourselves. Once we realize that, we sometimes aren't so willing to do these things. That's okay.

Each of us has boundaries on how far we are willing to go to achieve a goal. You need to recognize these boundaries up front so you won't set yourself up for "failure" trying to create something you're not willing to do your part in bringing about.

Take Action:

Go back to your wish list once more. Again, go over each item you wish to create for yourself.

Ask yourself the following questions:

- What steps will I have to take in order to bring this about?

- Once I have created this situation, what will I need to do to keep it?

- What will I have to change about myself in order to reach this goal?

Finally, of course, answer honestly whether you are willing to do whatever it takes to create the desire. If not - write down what you are willing to do.

If you find you are not willing to make necessary changes - or do the necessary work - don't despair. Simply take your desire down a notch. Adjust what you are asking for to a level where you are willing to do whatever it takes. This accomplishes the purpose of helping you not to give up when you reach a point where you are not willing to move forward.

Again - I am not asking you to settle for less. You will find that, as these lesser desires manifest, you willingness to do more will increase. As that happens, you may raise the level of your desires back to their original place.

Now you have one final - and necessary - set of questions to ask yourself about the desires on your list.

Take Action:

Return to your list and go over each item one more time. Ask yourself the following questions. At first, it may seem obvious the answers to questions 2 and 3 are, "No." Think deeply. Be absolutely certain that is the correct answer.

- What am I going to do with it when I get it?

- Will this harm anyone - either physically, mentally or emotionally?

- Will this take away from - or deprive - someone else of anything?

When creating circumstances for our lives we must be sure what we create will not bring harm or loss to anyone else. If it does, harm or loss will surely come back to us sooner or later - possibly in very dramatic ways.

Affirmations

Although we aren't quite ready to use affirmations as such, it's time to begin thinking about them. Nearly every teacher who instructs on using creative energies - or positive mental attitude - also teaches affirmations.

An affirmation is a positive phrase or statement. We are making a positive statement to affirm something is true. Usually affirmations are used repeatedly in an attempt to "trick" the unconscious mind into believing them.

Do affirmations work? Well, yes - and no. Depends on how you do it.

Vast numbers of people have been taught to use affirmations by repeating a positive statement over - and over - and over. The idea is to convince your unconscious mind of the truth of the statement. You can certainly learn your multiplication tables that way but rarely will you will bring what you want into your life.

Words do not create. Feelings create!

When you repeat a statement over and over - it becomes hypnotic. Ever been to a Catholic wake where the Rosary was said? Only the most devout can repeat those prayers that many times without thinking about something else while they do it. Devotion is a feeling. Feeling or emotion will always hold your attention.

You must bring your *attention* to the things you wish to create for your life. Later in *The MASTER COURSE*, I'll be giving you a couple of better ways to affirm what you want. They take a bit more time than just parroting words but they are astoundingly effective.

For now, I'd like to help you understand affirmations better. I don't want you to jump ahead of me and begin using them ineffectively.

Some people believe it doesn't matter whether or not you "pay attention to the words" when using affirmations. These are the same people who believe you can trick your unconscious mind. You can't. Not with affirmations at any rate.

Remember, the unconscious mind is the feeling mind. It only retains - and acts upon - what is presented to it with feeling. Obviously, little or no feeling is involved in mindlessly repeating statements.

The belief you hold, which is opposite to the affirmation you are using, is firmly planted. It was planted with feeling or you wouldn't be creating along those lines. The new ideas must be implanted with even more feeling in order to oust the old beliefs.

Your unconscious mind hears many statements every single day. It also ignores the biggest part of them. Unless your feelings are triggered, the ideas behind the statements will have no effect on you.

People have spent untold amounts of money for subliminal tapes that repeat affirmations during sleep. Ask someone who has used them if they worked. If the answer is, "Yes," ask them how long it lasted. If the answer to that question is that the results did last, the chances are the recorded voice on the tape was stating the affirmations with a great deal of feeling. Those feelings were somehow transferred to the one listening to the tapes. *Those* tapes, by the way, are worth their weight in gold!

This is one of the most important things you can learn about using creative energies. No power exists in affirmations. The power is in the feeling behind the affirmation. Later in the Course, we will learn how to charge your affirmations with feeling.

Beliefs About Wealth

The thing more people wish to create than anything else is wealth. Money. More money. The basic desire is actually a wish for a higher standard of living. Since it does take money in our modern societies to buy material things - it's logical to create money.

Although we are able to create whatever we desire, we will only manifest those things we believe we can have. We must believe we can have more money before money will come to us. This isn't always as easy as it seems.

You may look around and see people who are manifesting fistfuls of cash. You may wonder, "If so many other people can do it, why can't I?" The answer is in the question.

"... Why can't I," is the problem. The very asking of the question indicates a belief that you can't do it. That belief needs to be changed!

You probably have many years of carrying the burden of that belief around with you - weighing you down - crushing your attempts at financial prosperity. You may also find other beliefs supporting the idea you "can't do it." Where did you get those ideas?

You may be able to reason these unfortunate beliefs are not true. You know that. You really know that! You can think it through and know you deserve every good thing. So, why do the beliefs continue to influence what you create when you know you have changed your mind?

Beliefs are based in feeling! It isn't your rational thoughts that go out to create for you. It's your feelings that determine what you will manifest. Feelings create! Belief systems are very firmly rooted. They may go back to childhood. They are very often completely unconscious.

Listen to the thoughts in your mind and you will find your true beliefs concerning your chances for wealth. Look for the beliefs you have been holding telling you that you don't deserve to have the wealth you desire. Then, change them to something more positive. Withdraw the energy of fear and replace it with feelings of positive expectation.

Know you do deserve every good thing! No person on the planet inherently deserves to have any more than any other person. It is your birthright to have it all! Please work with getting the *feeling* of this!

Feel the joy of having it before it comes! Be happy knowing you do deserve it. Feel grateful that you can have it all. Those are the feelings that will create what you want.

Take Action:

Picture yourself already having something you want. It can be anything at all. Create an image in your mind like a movie. See yourself enjoying this desire of yours. What are you doing with it? Live with it - love it - see yourself expressing joy that it is yours.

As you do this, involve yourself completely in the feelings you would be experiencing if this image were true right now. Do this often even if for a short period of time. Let those feelings become real.

As you do the action technique above, you will be creating new feelings around your desires. You may have been told what you wish for can never be yours. You have many feelings around that belief.

With this simple visualization process, you are creating new feelings around this same desire. Allow yourself to let these new positive feelings have full rein. Experience those feelings as intensely as you can. And, while you're at it - create some feelings of joy that the old beliefs are unfounded. They were merely a judgment on the part of someone else. They have nothing to do with what you can have!

Choosing Wealth

In Part Two of *The MASTER COURSE*, we learned the first in a 7-step process for creating wealth. This was called, "creating a void." We had to clean up and clean out those things taking up space where we wanted new wealth to be demonstrated. We were creating an empty space for the universe to fill.

Now, we must decide what we want to fill that space. We must choose!

You may be surprised to learn an expectation of being poor is a choice to be poor. It may be an unconscious choice but it is a choice nevertheless.

Once you learn to identify your unconscious choices, you may make another choice at the conscious level. You may identify these unconscious choices by looking at your "automatic" expectations. These are the ones you never think much about.

Take Action:

Make a list of all your expectations regarding wealth and financial security. Write down the first thought that comes into your mind when you think of having all the money you want.

Wherever you find a negative idea regarding your chances of being rich, replace it with a different choice. Write down the new choice and begin to consciously expect those circumstances to come into your life.

Even if you can't believe it at first – make yourself feel the feeling of expectation of the positive outcome. Understand this technique to be a way of making a conscious choice to change your expectations.

As you do the action technique above, don't allow yourself to get caught up in all the reasons why you have come to expect less than total financial security. Those are only the causes of your current expectations. The fact that something happened once does not mean it must happen every time. The expectation it will happen again is what creates a same or similar situation to happen a second time.

Remember, we are not dealing with logic here. We are dealing with the energies of feelings. Those feelings can - and will - create beyond all logic.

Choosing wealth is sometimes one of the most difficult choices to make. Many of us have had the evils of money drummed into us from an early age. Even if that's not the case, we also deal with our issues as to whether we deserve to be wealthy. Or, whether it's possible for us.

Any previous experience of perceived lack only serves to reinforce our expectations of there never being enough. You may have years and years of "proof" you will never have your dreams of financial security. Would you believe me if I told you that you created that proof?

You did. You created it by expectations implanted in you from an early age - or from just that first unfortunate experience of failure. We carry tons of feelings surrounding these circumstances.

Here is a perception that needs to be changed when you begin to create wealth for yourself. The idea of "failure." The perception of the meaning of "failure" can be changed to "redirection." You didn't fail - you were redirected. No - I'm not reaching with this concept. Use the following technique and prove it to yourself.

Take Action:

Write down a time when you felt you had failed at something – maybe a business enterprise – a job – something to do with your finances.

Now move your memory past that point in time to what came later. Look for something that happened which could never have happened if you had succeeded. It may not have happened right away. You may have to move forward a bit in time to find it.

Look hard enough and you will find you were in fact - redirected - by the apparent failure. Even if we are redirected to a situation we find painful, sooner or later some good will come of it.

It will serve you well to spend a lot of time on this action technique. Follow every "failure" you ever experienced until you come to the point where you can see that it was a redirection.

This is one of the ways you can deal with any fear you can never make the choice for wealth. You may have a fear that your expectations will stay in the old poverty-consciousness rut. Bottom line?

There is no such thing as failure! Choose for success!

Be sure to do the action techniques thoroughly in every instance where your desire pertains to your financial well-being. So many people never enjoy the wealth which is naturally theirs simply because they have never answered the questions that will show them what they truly want.

For instance, if you wish to be wealthy but aren't willing to do whatever it takes to achieve that state - then, your choice is not for wealth. Your choice is for not doing something. Yes - choice can be quite complicated! And, never more so than when it comes to wealth.

If you are working toward financial prosperity, separate all desires from the original list you made referring to wealth, and put them on another list. Re-do each exercise - going ever deeper with your answers.

When you are finished with all your answers, review the list. Now - make adjustments. If too much seems to stand in the way of you actually achieving the level of wealth you first wrote down - adjust your desire to something more manageable.

This isn't settling for less! This is simply moving your desires into line with what you feel you can manage at first. You must be able to believe you can actually manifest what you desire.

This is a training course. We start at one point and end up at a point farther down the road. Think of it as your road to wealth. Take it one step at a time. With each step you can take successfully, your willingness to do more will expand. Your beliefs of what is possible for you will also expand.

Don't set yourself up to get lost on the road. Use your map. Go from Point A to Point B. Create small successes that will allow you the confidence to build larger successes.

Be sure you give serious consideration to, "Be careful what you ask for." The rest of that thought is, "For you will surely get it."

Before you choose, think carefully about the possible ramifications of having what you want. This isn't negative thinking. It is merely following through the entire scenario of what might happen when your desire is created.

In some cases this way of looking forward can help you avoid pitfalls down the line. You don't necessarily need to change your desire. Simply be sure you choose in such a manner that you can handle whatever might come to you along with the manifestation.

Choose carefully - very carefully.

Stressing Your Health

CREATING our own physical well-being is one of the most difficult concepts to convey. We don't seem to question that we can control it to some extent with things in the outer. We understand that "eating right" - exercise - rest, etc. have great influence in maintaining health.

The more difficult part is convincing students they also have "inner" influence. Even recent publicity regarding mind/body control is sometimes scoffed at by those who believe their only choices lie in following the dictates of those medical professionals who still believe one has nothing to do with the other.

Yet, it's no secret nearly all disease is based in stress. What is stress but the inner? Conditions in the outer may contribute to the stress. What we don't always stop to think about is how much stress is created by our inner expectations.

First let's take a look at the two types of stress. We have stress - and we have eustress. Eustress is what we might call "good stress." Yet, its effects are exactly the same as "bad stress."

I'm sure I don't need to define "stress" for you. Eustress is the stress created by happy events: anticipation of a vacation - preparations for a wedding - starting an exciting new project - opening your own business - awaiting the birth of a child. All happy situations, which produce "eustress."

Eustress comes from excitement or anticipation. These feelings do the same things to the body as stress does. The nervous system reacts in the same way - and the results are the same. Unwelcome stress is put upon the cells of the body.

Both stress and eustress are fear-based - even though eustress comes about through happy situations. It isn't difficult to isolate the fear behind any stress. You'll see it with very little contemplation. The fear behind eustress is a bit harder to identify.

When we are experiencing eustress, it is in anticipation of an event we are looking forward to with pleasure. So, where does fear enter the scene? It's a fear that things won't go as well as we would like.

It's unfortunate that, even when we are expecting happy times, we still live with fear. Earlier, I mentioned fear comes from two places: fear we won't get something we want and fear we'll lose something we already have. The fear behind eustress is often both.

This fear can be either conscious or unconscious. Let's use examples of both.

You might be preparing to take a long needed vacation. The conscious fear is fairly obvious.

- "What if something happens, and I don't get to go?"

- "What if I miss my flight?"

- "What if the travel agency didn't get the reservations done correctly?"

- "What if I get there and I don't have the proper clothes with me?"

- "What if it rains the whole time I'm there?

You get the picture, right? The unconscious fear, however, might not be so clear or obvious?

You may have memories of vacations that were a disaster. You may have memories of vacations where everyone was miserable. These might even be childhood memories you've forgotten all about - at the conscious level.

Let's take another example:

You have received a promotion at your job - or you are about to open your own business. The obvious fears might be:

- "What if I'm not ready to do the job?"

- "What if I can't present the "right" image?"

- "What if I find I don't like the work?"

- "What if I have to work longer hours?"

Obvious, right? Yet, once again, you may also have unconscious fears going on. Again, they will probably be manifesting from memories. You may have a memory of someone saying you would never measure up. You may even have a memory of some perceived failure in the past. Maybe someone close to you took this kind of chance and failed.

It can seem impossible to escape stress in one form or another. This is why I teach living with fear rather than living in fear. Stressful situations move us forward so we really don't want to avoid them altogether. As you can see by now, we would also have to avoid happy occasions.

Take Action:

This action technique must be used over and over in each stressful situation you encounter. The object is to identify the underlying fear which is bringing about the stress. You might try it just for practice on a situation you have already experienced.

Anytime you are "stressed out," you will first want to decide, is this stress - or eustress? The only reason to label it is that you may be anticipating a happy occasion. You may not understand why you feel so much stress when you "shouldn't" be.

Next - look for the fear. You will find the fears easily simply by listening to the words going through your head. They may be your own words - or they may be words that have been spoken to you in the past.

Once you have identified the true underlying fear, ask yourself - is it appropriate? What are the chances of that happening at all? Fear actually comes from our anticipation of events rather than the events themselves. Enjoyment can be completely ruined by the anticipation of some disaster. Our fear feelings are always based in anticipated loss of one kind or another.

Finally - return to the principles of spirit. Once these principles are thoroughly learned and internalized, fear will melt away. You'll find your periods of stress are magically reduced.

Since stress is so hard on the body - and since it will in fact bring on illness and disease - the greatest thing you can do toward creating perfect health is to reduce all stress. Both kinds!

I've already given you the most valuable tool for accomplishing that. In the Appendix of this book, you will be given a simple meditation/relaxation exercise. I trust you will use it daily. Any type of meditation will enormously reduce your stress load. It does incredible things for the body in just 20 minutes day. In fact, it's been *proven* to strengthen the immune system.

The body itself can't tell the difference between stress and eustress. The physical effects are exactly the same. Do I want you to give up your excitement over happy occasions? Of course not. I would like to have you learn how to manage eustress so it doesn't rock the world of your body's cells. I would like to have you learn how to *decide* what stress - and eustress - will do to your body.

I know, beyond a shadow of a doubt, how much influence choice has on our physical well-being. In the next chapter, I will tell you the story of how I learned the simplest creative technique of all.

A Short Story

When I was 6 years old, I had been ill with one ailment or another for most of two years. Although some of the common childhood diseases accounted for part of that time, most of it was miscellaneous this and that. I had throat problems, ear problems, fevers, headaches, stomach problems - you name it - I had it.

None of it was terribly serious but in those days things were done a bit differently than they are done today. A sick child was kept in bed and, depending upon the illness, it was often in a darkened room. We were fed disgusting things like milk toast and broth! Not a lot of fun. The diet itself could make you sick.

Each evening during the periods when I was confined to my bed, my father would come into my room to spend time with me. He read to me - helped me with the schoolwork I had to do at home - talked with and listened to me.

The following is a conversation we had one evening when I was quite upset over being ill so much of the time. I remember it clearly - and verbatim - because it has had such a dramatic effect on my life.

Child: I'm tired of staying in bed. I can't do anything I want to, and I hate being sick!

Father: I know. I don't like being sick either.

Child: How do you know? You're never sick!

Father: That's right and it's because I don't like it.

Child (whining): When am I going to get well again and stay well?

Father: Just as soon as you get tired enough of it, and make up your mind not to be sick any more.

Child: Is that what you did?

Father: That's exactly what I did.

Such a simple little conversation! With such far reaching implications.

I thought about what my father had said. Something told me if one person can do something - everyone can do it. I didn't doubt for a minute that he did it - therefore, so could I.

Before I went to sleep that night, my decision was made. No processes - no deep thinking - just a decision. I really was sick of being sick so I had a lot of feeling involved in this decision. I was determined. I would stop being ill.

No miraculous recovery occurred the next day but then, I hadn't asked for one. I didn't realize I could have stopped the illness in its tracks too. My decision was that when I got over this illness (I don't remember what it was) I would stop being sick!

And, that's exactly what happened.

Now, some might think this was a coincidence (which by the way, doesn't exist) and I was simply ready to outgrow childhood illness. I might even wonder about it myself if it weren't for my experiences ever since. I have been exposed to many, many communicable diseases since that time - without any sign of taking on the illness.

Just on a very common note, try taking care of four children, all with intestinal flu at the same time - and coming through it without a sign of the illness. In fact, over one Thanksgiving holiday, I had six children (from 1 to 9 years old) and three other adults in the house - all with intestinal flu. It was so bad, three of them had it twice over a five-day period.

Except me. I escaped untouched. All I have to do is remind myself that those "germs" have no effect on me. I simply don't allow it.

I know, I know - I make it all sound so simple. For me, it was simple. I was quite young when the decision was made - I had it on the best possible authority (my father) that it was possible - and I wasn't getting a single positive perk out of being ill.

I do have one area of physical distress. When I go to certain locations, I will develop a sinus condition. Interestingly, these are places where I am sometimes required to go - and where I especially do not want to be. I know the entire time the condition will right itself as soon as I can leave. It always does.

Am I doing this to myself? You bet! Why? I don't know. It's never been bad enough to cause me to make it stop. I believe it's a kind of verification for me that I need to get out of that location. I even believe I enjoy the validation of my feelings.

Earlier in this book, I discussed having asthma attacks – and how I overcame them. Interestingly, I didn't consider those attacks an illness. They sneaked up on me, and I simply thought of them as something making me not be able to breathe.

I had breathing problems again several years ago. I was considerably older by then. This time, it took me longer to get things under control, and I did have to have some medical intervention. I was told the condition would never get better!

Oh, how wrong they were! It did take my cells a while to completely recover, but recover we did. Now, the pulmonologist just shakes his head. The oxygen level in my blood went back to – and stays - completely normal.

Choosing Health

As with all areas of our lives, at some level we are making choices about how life is going to be for us. These choices are based in an expectation - an old belief - or even a judgment. Usually, the choices are unconscious. As always, the trick is to make conscious choices - and back them up with feeling!

"I don't know." This would be the answer to the question of why I was repeatedly ill for the two years prior to the conversation with my father. I would have to give you the same answer if you ask me why babies become ill - or are born ill. I don't know.

I have a theory but this isn't the appropriate place to discuss it. Here we are only interested in what you can do - once you reach an age where conscious decisions can be made.

Take Action:

Go through your memory banks and find memories of times when you were ill. This will be very specialized for each person and their personal experiences.

Choose a period of illness and examine it closely. Why were you ill? Did you expect to be? Was it the result of a virus you expected to be communicable? Was it the result of something you did - or didn't do - which you believe has a bearing on that particular ailment? Was it an illness you have repeatedly?

Think about what may have truly caused the illness. Is there a mind/body connection? Are you willing to accept the idea that your unconscious expectations can cause illness?

If not - and you truly want to be able to take control of your physical well-being - go deeper. You will need to accept - even embrace - this idea if you are to be successful.

We don't need to know consciously when we have been exposed to a virus or bacteria in order to keep it from affecting us. The cells already have their instructions and they will manifest according to our beliefs. Here are the instructions they have most likely received: "If a virus or bacteria comes into our space, we will accept the illness it brings." The cells recognize the invader whether we do or not. They know what to do.

Universal principles tell us spirit is life - spirit is power. You have life - therefore power - in your mind as well as in your body. And remember - the cells of your body actually contain mind - and therefore, intelligence.

The next thing we need to understand about choices for health is why we make some choices at all. If our choices are not automatic (based on beliefs and expectations) we may unconsciously choose ill health for at least two other reasons.

The first is that we are getting something out of it. We recognize some reward in being under the weather. It could be many things. It may be we get some kind of positive attention we fail to get in other ways. Many children become ill for this reason.

It may even be this is the only way we give ourselves the positive attention we need. The only time we can justify taking care of ourselves - due to still other beliefs and judgments.

There can be many, many, perceived rewards in being ill. Again, this may be all unconscious. The reward may even be in avoidance.

This is the opposite side of the coin. Rather than receiving something in being ill - or even unhealthy in general - we may use illness to avoid something. Maybe it's as simple as needing a couple of days off from work. Ooops! Feel a cold coming on! And there's always, "Not now, I have a headache!" And, it's a real headache.

It could also be more complicated. I know a woman who kept herself nearly at death's door for years because she didn't like to clean house. What about your friend who became suddenly ill just before the high school reunion? Or the brother who started having dizzy spells requiring an MRI (which found nothing) when it was time to help you move?

Avoidance of some kind is one of the most prevalent reasons for illness!

Take Action:

You knew it was coming. Time to review every illness you've experienced in your adult life. We do these reviews so you can find what you will need to stop doing in order to make new conscious decisions. You may include accidents if you like.

Take each experience of illness individually. Examine it closely and find the answers to some simple questions.

- What did I stand to gain?

- What did I manage to avoid?

- What was the basic reward? In other words - what did I truly need?

I can't impress upon you enough how important it is to find the answers to these questions. You simply cannot make new choices until you find out what the payoff was for the old choices.

Take Action:

After you have completed the action technique above, answer the following questions. It will do no good to answer these questions until you have found the rewards in being less than physically perfect.

- What am I willing to give up in exchange for perfect health?

- What am I willing to do to achieve perfect health?

Now, don't answer, "Anything!" to the second question. If I were to tell you (which I won't), you would have to run a mile every day for the rest of your life you might say, "Fine, I'll do it." But, what if I said you would have to run 20 miles? Find your limits on willingness.

Speaking of accidents ...

There are no accidents! Nothing can happen to us without our permission. Nothing. Even if an accident causes "death," at some level we have agreed to it.

In the case of us leaving this world, most of the time the level where this is decided is at the spiritual level. We would be completely unaware of it. This doesn't mean, though, we can't make another - conscious - decision.

Accidents that only harm rather than kill are also not "accidents." These usually come from the unconscious level. For instance ...

I have a friend who was maybe not as graceful as other children. As a child, he was told over and over that he was "clumsy." In adulthood, he is a walking accident. He trips - he falls - he smashes his thumb with a hammer - he runs into furniture - he drops things.

But - he only does these things when a member of his family of origin is around. It happens in front of the people he was embarrassed in front of as a child. I have watched him at other times and he moves more gracefully than most people. It's all unconscious - brought up only when he's afraid he'll be clumsy.

Something in the mind always causes an accident. And as you can see above - once again, it's fear. Fear creates accidents!

Nearly everyone has experienced something like this ... You are walking up some stairs, carrying something you can't see over, and you have the thought, "I hope I don't trip on these steps." You have just expressed fear. So, unless you are very careful after that - and consciously reject that fear - chances are you will trip before you get to the top of the stairs. Instant manifestation!

We have all experienced similar events. It is the natural order of things. We create everything with feelings. Certainly not always instantly, but we do create it. Hence, my statement: "There are no accidents." Eliminate fear through embracing the universal principles - and you'll eliminate accidents.

Balance & Control

BALANCE and control are the keys to creating your own perfect health. You may wonder why I would say that after just telling you your mind controls your body. Principle of Oneness! Mind and body are *One!* Balance and control of the mind is the very same thing as balance and control of the physical body.

You can achieve balance and control of the body by exercising in your mind. This was discussed in Part One of *The MASTER COURSE*. It is done through visualization.

Visualization, however, isn't terribly effective if you can't focus the mind. If you have "mind-chatter" going on while you are trying to visualize your body in a certain condition, your mind is neither balanced, nor in control.

Everything works both ways. If you can create a balanced, controlled body with your mind - you can create a balanced, controlled mind with your body. Everything in life needs to stay balanced if it is to work at optimum levels.

I know many disciplines from different parts of the world are designed for balance and control. I will briefly touch on two. Yoga - and Tai Ch'i. These may be the best known - and therefore, most acceptable for you to try.

Although many would disagree with me, I do not suggest either are necessary to achieve perfect health. They simply assist in training the mind - through use of the body - in balance and control. What I will say is this: the use of these disciplines will make all of your creative efforts more effective. They connect you to all the balanced energies of life.

Although both Yoga and Tai Ch'i are spiritual disciplines used for centuries, they are also excellent ways to tone the body. You can easily find classes for beginners at most community centers. You don't need to strive for transcendence to reap their value.

Either of these disciplines far outweighs strenuous physical exercise in their value for reducing stress on the cells of your body. Strenuous physical exercise has the exact same physical effects on the body as stress. Unless you are exercising for body building purposes, the results of certain types of Yoga - or Tai Ch'i - will give you the same results as strenuous exercise - without the accompanying stress.

Both Yoga and Tai Ch'i are based in balance and control of the body and mind. There is no separation. Balance, control and flexibility of the body will result in the same for the mind. *Provided* the exercises done toward that end are done from a position of inner peace.

I don't mean to imply that Yoga and Tai Ch'i are the only disciplines that will achieve the spectacular results of exercise without stress. Many other similar disciplines are available and being taught regularly. Find one you personally enjoy.

What Is True Love?

The preparation for creating loving relationships can be a long process. Here we're dealing with lots of history in the most intimate area of our lives - the area where we are most vulnerable. It comes from the history of our childhood as well as a possible history of unsatisfactory relationships.

In fact, we may be dealing with so much history, we either never learned - or have forgotten - what love is. We touched on this a bit in an earlier chapter. Now we need to go into it more deeply. This will be necessary before you can make good choices.

When we wish to bring a lasting relationship into our lives, we do still need to make choices before we start. Remember, you will create exactly what you expect. If, deep down, you expect certain things of a relationship, you will attract exactly the kind of person who will give them to you. You need to make your expectations conscious.

In Part Four, we'll deal with letting go of the feelings from past relationships that were less than ideal. It's best to keep those feelings for now so you'll have something to compare with fulfilling relationships.

Attitude is everything. It can limit us - or empower us. The following are concepts that improve attitudes toward relationships in general. Work with each concept until you begin to get a feel for it.

Believe in yourself!

Never look back. Leave the past where it belongs - in the past. Don't compare your success in relationships with others or beat yourself up because of past history. Get past any fear you may have that you'll never get it right. Remember, defeat is a wonderful teacher. Take the lesson gratefully - and leave the rest.

I don't care what your past history is. You can have a fulfilling intimate relationship! Please know that for yourself. It may take a bit of courage to try but, haven't you heard? "Courage" is: *feeling the fear and doing it anyway!*

Accept love as a celebration of humanness!

Not perfection. Each person is a unique human being. We must celebrate that in ourselves - and in others.

The true "love of your life" will rarely be just like you. Holding out for someone who is the "same" as you, will keep you looking for a long, long time. What you want is a unique person with whom you can celebrate your differences - rather than criticizing them and causing endless conflict.

Love from your spirit!

The ego is in the brain - the spirit is in the heart. Yes - we do need to do the head work ahead of time - ask ourselves all the questions - and find our own answers. After that, we need to trust the heart.

If you have given your heart too quickly in the past - without doing the head work first - you may have thought you were in love several times. Each time, it may have ended painfully. When that happens, we begin to equate love with pain. Pain equals ego. This isn't love.

Love is energy!

It's the most powerful force in the universe. The energy of love has a particular vibratory frequency - and can be measured. It is, in fact, the highest frequency. A good relationship is a mutual exchange of this love energy.

Energy moves. Love moves! You want your love to move. You want it to grow. When love grows, the partnership grows. If you don't grow with your partner, your love will stagnate.

Love must have clarity!

Observe two people who claim to be in love when they have a difference of opinion on an issue vital to each of them. Positions are taken.

Either may try to push past the other to get what is important to them. It may be done emotionally - yelling and screaming. It may be done intellectually - arguing in defense of their own positions. Others, who don't believe in getting angry, may begin to say things in a veiled way - or do things in a very underhanded way.

This is not love. These are forms of anger and resentment. The love energy stops and the fear energy begins.

Truly loving partners will make a third party of the issue involved rather than each making it an extension of the self. They will then work together on the issue to find a resolution mutually satisfying to both. This effectively prevents the issue from becoming a part of the relationship.

Love is not a light bulb!

It isn't something you can turn on and off. You can't have it one day - and not the next. That's emotion! Emotion is never consistent. Love is energy! *Positive energy*. It is always consistent. We must follow a path where we use that energy in the way it is intended.

Love yourself first!

You can't give away what you don't have. We are loving when we can feel compassion and understanding. If we don't have that for ourselves - how will we give it to others?

All judgment of the self has to stop. Only then can we embody the love energy. We must embody that energy within ourselves before we can send it out into the universe to attract its complementary energy. This is the most basic - and important - requirement for creating a good relationship.

Trust and truth are essential!

Love has many components but these two are mandatory. It isn't always easy because we may be afraid on both counts. Issues definitely come up when we are starting new relationships. All of our beliefs about ourselves - and the world - determine what we can give to another. Our other relationships do affect our romantic relationships!

Love takes patience!

In fact, love *is* patience. Love has no need to run willy-nilly right into every possible relationship that presents itself. If you think it's "love at first sight," think again. Carefully. It's the attraction of like energies! Those energies may - or may not be - love.

Choosing Intimacy

As with all other areas of life transformation, the next step is to choose. Would you believe me if I told you - at some level - you may not even want an intimate relationship? Probably not, but it's true nevertheless.

Whatever is manifesting in our lives at any given moment is due to choices we have made – the expectations we hold. If you are alone right now, rest assured; you are not being slighted by the universe in any way.

You are alone because at some level you have chosen to be alone at this time. It's part of the learning you have programmed for yourself. You may make a different choice tomorrow.

Once again, we must make a definitive choice for what we want before attempting to create a lasting relationship. We covered our willingness to *do* and our willingness to *give* in Part II. Now, we need to begin the choice of what we *want*. What we do here are the basics. You'll find, when you begin the work in Part Four, your choices will expand.

The most basic choice is mentioned above. *Is this what you want?* We all have a longing in our soul to be with another person who understands us totally and accepts us unconditionally. There's no doubt about that. We are even led to believe this person must be one with whom we are in an intimate relationship. In truth, this person could just as easily be our best friend - a sibling - even a parent.

Of course, it would be ideal to find this in a life-mate. It's even possible. You can create it. But, do you want it? How much are you willing to commit? When are you willing to commit? For how long?

Is there something coming up next year that could have an effect on a new relationship? For instance, are you in line for a promotion and/or a long-distance transfer? Would a relationship now create other decisions for you later that could be uncomfortable?

We truly often say we would like to be in a relationship when, in fact, we don't want that at all. We may not even realize this. Not to have an intimate relationship is a perfectly acceptable choice. To want to find that relationship "later" is a perfectly acceptable choice.

Sometimes, when we want it "now," we don't stop to realize all it will entail - at least not at a conscious level. Unconsciously we are making decisions that keep us from searching out the relationship. We might not recognize it if it were right in front of us. The unconscious mind has its own agenda.

Ambivalence is an attitude that often gets into the picture. For instance, maybe you have been alone for a while. Maybe you even disliked it intensely when it began. Yet, as time passed, you may have seen the advantages.

You have no one to consider but yourself. You have absolute freedom in every area of your personal life. Even when loneliness begins to play a role, we tend to balance what would be gained from a relationship by what would be lost. Again, this may be purely unconscious.

Before we set about creating your lasting relationship - which we will do in Part Four - you will need to be sure this is what you want. And, you will need to be sure *when* you want it. The creative process will bring you what you ask for. You don't want to find out later you weren't ready after all.

Take Action:

Take a good long look at your life situation at this moment. Think about where you are – and where you might be in a year. Think about what you are hoping for. Answer the following questions:

- Is it possible I am I bowing to what's expected of me - rather than having a true desire for a relationship right now?

- Is there anything on the horizon that might possibly affect a relationship if I had one? What is it?

- What could happen to a relationship if my life changes after the relationship begins? (Follow this train of thought all the way to its conclusion.)

- Am I enjoying absolute freedom in my personal life right now?

- Would I feel closed off or restricted if I didn't have absolute freedom anymore?

- Do I have any residual fear from a past relationship causing me to hesitate to try it again?

- Have I been exposed to a seriously unhappy relationship of someone else's - and do I have any fear about being caught in the same situation?

- Do I have any concern I might have to give up too much of myself in an intimate relationship?

- Do I have others in my life who would be affected by my relationship - and what are all my thoughts around that situation?

A "Yes" answer to any of these questions (except the third) may indicate you are not clear in whether you truly wish for a relationship right now. I often hear clients say, "Well, yes, but I could get over all that if the right person came into my life.

When asked to describe this "right person," these clients tend to draw a picture of absolute perfection. When asked what they believe the chances are of this perfect person showing up, they nearly always grin and say, "Zero."

The answer is in the grin. They have set up impossible standards for a life mate in an attempt to be sure they don't find him/her. This is an indication of the belief that we *should* want to be in relationship.

Please don't think I'm trying to talk you out of creating your lasting relationship with the material in this Course. Nothing could be further from the truth. If you are experiencing a longing in the soul to be part of a couple, by all means - go for it!

On the other hand, don't do it because you think you should - or because, "It would be kind of nice." Nice won't last long if you go into a relationship when you're not ready. Please consider the life of the other person you will be affecting by your decision. Nothing is so important as how we affect others with our creations.

The purpose of the next action technique is to try to get any unconscious fears you may have regarding relationships up into your conscious mind. Remember - the feelings around an unconscious fear may be creating a lack of relationship. Once a fear becomes conscious, it's easier to deal with. You will probably find some unconscious fears are totally irrational. These can be discarded with some concentrated rational thinking. They may then be replaced with the truth of the matter.

Take Action:

Give yourself some private, peaceful time to do this exercise. Stay relaxed. Write down every single fear you have about entering into a long-term intimate relationship.

The conscious ones will come first. As you slow down, begin to picture yourself in a relationship. See what pops into your mind. Don't push yourself. Just let the thoughts come out on paper as they will.

Now, go over each fear. Is it rational? Is it a real fear? Is it something you are willing to give up? Is it something you can think of a solution for if it were to actually happen?

Fear must be eliminated as much as possible when attempting to create a relationship. If it isn't, the fears will bring you what you do not want. You may be able to eradicate a lot of fear by simple preparation. Decide ahead of time what you can do if your fear does come before you.

Are You Ready?

You may feel in your heart you're ready for a committed relationship and normally, I tell people to follow their hearts. In such an important area as sharing your life with another human being, it takes more than that. You may feel ready - you may find a person you feel you can love - you may be about to jump right in without a backward glance. The relationship may even last for a while.

The truth is - for the long-term - you may need to cultivate certain characteristics within yourself. You need to be sure you are ready and able to sustain a long-term relationship.

Take Action:

Ask yourself the following questions and see if you need to expand your own characteristics in some areas.

Am I willing to let go of issues standing in the way of my growth - or the growth of a relationship?

We must be willing to make reasonable adjustments within any relationship. If there is any area where you are not comfortable, you may need to work on your own motivations and issues.

Am I willing to accept problems for what they are and move through them rather than terminating a relationship prematurely?

I know many folks prefer to see problems as challenges. Yet a challenge indicates someone must win. A problem is just that - a problem to be solved. How are your problem-solving skills? How quick are you to run away from a problem rather than working on a solution?

Do I believe in myself and in my own ability to form a loving, healthy relationship?

If we don't believe in ourselves - and our abilities - how can we expect to create a good relationship? The answer is - we can't! If your model for relationships has not been a positive one - find new models. Observe those who do well in their relationships. Educate yourself in the necessary skills until your self-confidence rises.

Can I gracefully accept change when life takes a new direction?

Even when we take full charge of creating our own lives, we may be confronted with changes beyond our control. The life changes of others can still affect us. Flexibility is a necessary ingredient in a successful and fulfilling relationship.

Am I patient?

This is probably self-explanatory. It takes time to build a successful relationship. It also takes the ability to be patient with situations - yourself - and always - with another person.

Do I have a positive mental attitude?

Persistent pessimism is a sure-fire killer for a good relationship. When life challenges present themselves, a positive and optimistic attitude is your best insurance for moving through them successfully.

Can I accept the personality characteristics of others?

It's important we be able to separate behaviors that are chosen - or deliberate - from behaviors that are inborn. Certain behaviors may be adjusted in favor of a relationship. Others will need to be accepted for what they are - and lived with. "My way or the highway," will end up on the road every time.

Am I willing and able to forgive?

Carrying a grudge has probably broken up more relationships than any other circumstance. People make mistakes. People make bad decisions. How capable are you of forgiveness? How willing are you to forgive and move forward without retribution?

The Priority

All relationships should be equal. Your partner's happiness is as important as yours. And vice versa. If your partner is unhappy, you will soon be unhappy, too. Yet, as mentioned previously - neither of you can make the other happy.

When decisions need to be made, often two people will see the situation differently - and wish to handle it differently. Now is the time to consider the third entity in the relationship - the relationship itself.

Make the relationship the priority. Put the relationship first in all decisions. What is best for the relationship? What will support or enhance the overall partnership? When you put the relationship first, it's often easier to reach a compromise.

Needless to say, you will need to find another person who is willing to do these same things. You may think that won't be easy - but you also might be surprised. Don't settle for anything else. If you are willing to put a relationship first, you deserve to have a partner who is also willing.

Creating a relationship is relatively easy - whether it's bringing the right person into your life or improving a current relationship. Most of the work is preparatory. The "head work" needs to be done before the actual creative techniques are used.

Just remember as you are preparing yourself - and your life - to receive a partner, you are also actually creating the desired outcome. Once the right energies are being generated - the right partner will be attracted like a moth to flame.

Heading Off "Failure"

In Part Four, we'll begin using the techniques and processes that will create the desires of your heart. I can't impress on you enough how important it is that you thoroughly digest - and internalize - the first three Parts of *The MASTER COURSE* before you start. This means you need to be doing all of the action techniques on a regular basis.

Expecting all you need to do is read it, is a big mistake! Without the proper mind-sets, all the process techniques in the world won't work for you. It would be like trying to build a house without a foundation. One good wind and it will all come tumbling down.

I was once told I put "too much" in the first Parts of this Course. There's a reason for that. The basic ideas are being presented in many different ways. You are given many different ways of accomplishing the same things. You don't need detailed instructions on many of these ideas. It's the concept that is important.

I do that in the first three Parts of *The MASTER COURSE* to give you as many ways to understand - and change - your mind-sets as possible. All of the processes that follow in Part IV are dependent on your preparatory work through the first part of the Course. This is why the action techniques are so important.

Above all else your internalization of the principles of spirit from Part One will guarantee your success. If every thought, word and deed is filtered through those principles, you will understand completely why these life reviews and examinations of belief are necessary.

If you are reading this, I assume you may be wishing to transform some part of your life. Transformation takes time and - most of all - preparation. Remember the time that the caterpillar spends in the cocoon before the transformation into the butterfly is complete!

I have known people to go through creative processes and not receive what they were attempting to create. In fact, most books written on the subject will contain "disclaimers." These are the statements that release the author from any responsibility when something doesn't work. Those who have failed to bring about their desired creations also use disclaimers.

I'm going to give you all of the disclaimers here, but for a different reason. I'm going to show you they are bunk! There are no excuses!

Disclaimers used by the person who worked the process:

"My creation didn't manifest because I'm not worthy to have the things I really want."

Not worth it? Who are you? Are you not a child of the universe? Do you not create every day of your life? Are you not One with every person on the planet who creates the good stuff every day? Were you not taught these things by your teacher?

In this case, you have made a choice toward not having what you say you want.

"My creation didn't manifest because the universe is punishing me."

The universe punishes no one! We only punish ourselves and we do it fairly regularly. We can make another choice at any time.

"My creation didn't manifest because the universe doesn't want me to have it."

Write this down somewhere. *The universe does not care what you have!* Or, don't have. Nothing in the universe is set up to cause us pain or lack. It's strictly up to us how we manipulate the energies. We are doing the creating - or the non-creation.

Disclaimers used by teachers/authors:

"Your creation didn't manifest because you failed to wait for "divine ideas" to come to you."

There's judgment in the phrase, "divine idea." It indicates some ideas are "higher" than others. It indicates your ideas are less than ideas that come from some place "out there." It completely ignores the Principle of Oneness. All ideas are divine. Some simply fit certain situations better than others. The outer (out there) is no more divine than the inner (you).

We have all acted on ideas inappropriate to a situation at one time or another. Blaming failure to receive divine ideas is placing responsibility somewhere other than the self. It also creates the illusion of separation.

I know a story about a man who once manifested food for the multitudes. He didn't bless - or receive - a divine idea. He blessed - and received - fishes and loaves. Instantly. Those people could have starved to death on ideas.

"Your creation didn't manifest because the "divine timing" was off."

Divine timing is the instant you accept something. Not when something "out there" decides you can have it. You decide!

You might think of divine timing as your life plan, however. Look at it this way. If it's in your face - it's time to work on it. You decide. You accept. You create. Divine timing is always when you decide it will be.

"Your creation didn't manifest because you have hidden resentments and unforgiveness working against you."

First, let me say you certainly don't have to be made pure before you can manifest good in your life. That's nonsense. I've seen some pretty unsavory people do a fine of job of creating exactly what they want. No judgment exists in the creative energies.

Some truth, however, is contained in that statement. The negative energies of resentments and unforgiveness do keep you from being a clear channel for the good you seek. This does tend to slow things down. Yet, as always, intent and commitment are still the primary determining factors in your success.

I mention these things now - before we begin the processes in the next Part of *The MASTER COURSE* - to allow you to be prepared. You will be able to watch for allowing yourself excuses if things don't go easily the first time.

If something isn't working for you, it is for one of only two reasons.

The first reason is *you have not fully accepted what you desire*. Only you can go into your memory banks and find out why. This is what the action techniques in this Course are designed to help you do.

Usually it's just as simple as we can't fully believe everything that's possible for us. I tell you to believe it, and I did a healing on one eye, nothing short of miraculous (Part One). Yet, I still haven't been able to believe I can simply hold out my hand and have money (fishes and loaves) appear right in it.

The second true reason we sometimes fail to bring forth our intended creations is we are not using universal principles correctly. Universal laws are always at work. Yet, without correct use of the principles underlying the laws, the laws may bring forth something very different from our desire.

Let's use the law that states, "What goes out must come back." The primary principle involved is the Principle of Oneness; "What we give to others, we give to ourselves."

And, let's assume we are attempting to create wealth. One of the techniques you will learn for creating anything is you must give what you want to receive. Since we're creating wealth, we know we must give money to get money. So we give it - but we give it resentfully, feeling the whole time as if we can't afford to give it.

The law of cause and effect is set into motion. If we are giving fearfully, we are not using the Principle of Oneness properly. We are denying our belief that we are giving to ourselves. Rather than creating with the energy of giving with love - we create with the energy of fear of lack.

Of course, we do get back what we gave. More fear - resulting in more lack. All this comes straight from a failure to grasp, internalize and live by the universal Principle of Oneness.

My purpose for this closing chapter of Part Three has been twofold:

1) To alert you before we start on the processes in the next chapters as to why your acceptance of the universal principles is so important.

2) To forestall any excuse-making before it gets started. When we don't get instant gratification, we tend to rush to the conclusion we are failing. Then we start looking around for an excuse as to why this is so.

The chances are better than great you are not failing at all. Remember: you have been creating your life for years. Using these same techniques without even realizing it. Re-training is necessary! That's is why this Course was created to be worked on over a period of time. Don't be in a hurry to call it quits and start looking for an excuse.

Our creations are our own responsibility. Whatever they are. Use the universal principles correctly - believe in your own creative power - and success will be yours!

The work in Part Three has you looking for the underlying beliefs, expectations, and positions that help you decide what to create unconsciously.

If you find you are mired in self-doubt and/or negative ideas on any of the subjects discussed, go immediately back to the Workbook.

You have many action exercises in this Part. The questions in the exercises were designed to help you go deeper and more fully into the concepts needed to create in all parts of your life. Please be sure to do all action exercises fully and thoroughly.

Don't despair if you found more things you hadn't realized. This is why we take things slowly and step-by-step.

Take your time to explore everything in Part Three fully. By the time you've finished, you should be seeing yourself in a whole new light. Soon, you will be prepared to begin the actual creative process taught in Part Four.

Part Four

Introduction to Part Four

In the first three parts of *The MASTER COURSE* you have been presented with the principles of positive creation: the mind-sets needed and the preparatory work. All this was necessary if you hope to bring *lasting transformation* into any area of your life.

In Part Four, we will begin to learn the processes that will bring about your desired creations. These will be very specific tasks in each area of life - each with a definite purpose. *Remember to read every chapter!* The techniques are all interchangeable and you will pick up more information than if you read only the area you're interested in changing right now.

Sometimes, students experience nearly instant results in some areas. Usually, this is in the areas where they have the least fear. Never forget - you are creating your life - with your expectations - every moment of every day. You already know you can do it!

The problem is we so easily create what we do not want - because we've been doing it all our lives. We have believed what we were told - we have believed good things weren't possible for us - we have lacked confidence in ourselves and in the goodness of the universe. *Those mind-sets must be changed.*

The second reason we can create what we do not want is we expect that very thing to manifest. Expectation is one of the most powerful aspects of creation. What we expect - we get!

So, expect the best! You didn't spend money to buy this book for nothing. Put your money to work. Learn Parts One, Two and Three, and practice them until they become your new approach to life.

Learn the processes presented in Part Four so you will start doing them as second nature. These processes are very simple and have been taught over and over by many people. What people fail to learn is the processes won't work consistently unless you have mastered the material in the first three Parts of this Course.

I am going to show you the same basic process for all creative activities. I'll do it for each area of life - prosperity - health - and relationships. I will tailor it each time to the particular area of life involved, so you will have strong examples for each. Then, I'll give you some added directions for creating in all areas of life.

Do read how to create in all areas of life since points may be made in one area that aren't made in another. Get the full picture!

Follow the directions and you'll manifest the same good things that others who have taken - and used - this Course, have experienced.

At the end of Part Four, you'll find the goal we are approaching with *The MASTER COURSE*. If you relate these processes to the Universal Principles explained in Part One, you'll find - in time - you can surrender the processes altogether.

In that surrender, you will automatically - always - accept and receive all good things!

Ready to Begin

By now, I hope you have come to understand we create everything in our lives. We have been creating even things we do not want - either consciously or unconsciously - through our expectation of what it's possible for us to have. There is never a time when we are not creating.

All we are going to do from this point forward is create only *consciously*. We have, in fact, been using these same processes in creating all the things we didn't want!

Following, you will find the last things you need to be sure are done before beginning the creative processes. Be sure not to ignore these very important steps. They will go a long way toward assuring your success!

Letting Go

Old feelings are one of the most serious things blocking us from creating our desires. Old negative feelings: those resentments and feelings of anger - or outrage - we may have been harboring for years. These negative feelings create chaotic energies that will create the very things that reinforce those same old feelings.

To create positive and joyous experiences we must surround ourselves with positive energy - what I call the "Love Energy." This is the energy behind all positive feelings. Easier said than done? Not really. It just takes paying attention.

We all have happy things we can think about. Our thoughts are strictly our choice. When you find yourself in the midst of thinking old angry - or unhappy - thoughts, make another choice. Deliberately turn your thoughts to something that makes you feel happy. This will overcome negative energies and surround you with the positive energies you need to create positive situations.

Believe it, or not, the easiest way to do this is … When you catch yourself thinking angry or unhappy thoughts, simply tell yourself, "Stop!" Say it out loud at first. We are conditioned to obey the command, "Stop!" It's an automatic reaction to quit doing whatever we are doing when we hear the word.

Then, deliberately replace the thoughts with something that makes you feel happy. After you do this a few times, you'll be able to simply think the word, "Stop," and change your thoughts.

Another little trick is to stay in the present moment. The past is past. It can't be changed. Stop thinking backward and think about what you can do - right now - to create the desires of your heart. Clean your mental house! Let all that old stuff go - you need the space!

It's imperative to release the things taking up space in your life. Only then can the universe bring in your desired changes. You must first create a place for your newness to live. This not only applies to "things" - it applies to what is cluttering up our minds.

Create Your Space

In order to create the things we want in life, we must be able to feel the power of who we are. We need a space where we can recharge our own unique energy.

For the most part, we live in communal societies. We have family, friends, neighbors, and co-workers - all in our space. In fact, often we may feel like we have no space at all to call our own. It always seems necessary to adjust to the needs and energies of others.

Look around at what you think of as your own space. It might be your home. It might be your office. Wherever you spend your greatest amounts of time. What do you see? Is this place yours? Does it reflect your energy - or the energy of others? Do you like what you see? Do you feel completely comfortable there? If not - change it!

It may not be possible, at this point in your life, to have everything exactly the way you want it. You may have others to consider - and that's appropriate. But, you may be doing your own life creation under the influence of the energies of other people.

You must use your own energies - and only your own energies - to create the desires of your heart.

Find a space you can call your own. Try for a room. If that isn't possible, even a corner someplace will work. Make this space yours. Claim it as yours - and yours alone. Fill it with things you love. Your colors - your textures - your sounds - your scents - your treasured "stuff." Involve all of your senses in this space. Go to this space to recharge your energy.

This is your "feel good" place. It can be outside just as easily as inside. All the time that you spend in this place will help you to focus your most powerful creative energies.

Take Action:

Experience the energies of you. Make a space that belongs only to you – a space where you can rest and recharge – a space where you experience the peace of your own best energy. Then, create from the joy of that energy which is uniquely yours!

Open Your Mind

People often limit themselves when using creative techniques. We sometimes tend to have linear thinking when we need to "spread out."

We limit what the universe can bring us when we are too specific. We also bring about limitation by deciding what can be appropriate for us. Sometimes we limit our possibilities by clinging to old ideas and beliefs.

When you are bringing your desires into being through creative techniques, the mind needs to be wide open! Whatever you think may be the ideal - the universe may have a better - and higher - ideal. Possibilities beyond what you could even have dreamed.

If your mind isn't open to any possibilities other than those you have visualized for yourself, you may be shutting out even more wondrous outcomes. Don't trap yourself into thinking it isn't big enough. If you simply can't think of anything better, that's okay - as long as your mind is open.

When setting your intent - and making your commitment - for transformation, choose what you believe is the best outcome. Then make your statement for: "This, or something better." After that - trust the universe!

As author Richard Bach wrote:

"It is a huge mistake to limit the universe. Don't!"

Creative Energy

You've probably heard that your words and thoughts create the situations of your life. Not true.

Words are nothing more than the vehicle of energy. They carry energy out into the universe to find like energies. The only creative power of words is in the feeling behind the words.

Words spoken without feeling have no power whatsoever to create anything. Words spoken from fear - or from joy and expectation - carry all power to create the spoken situation. The words are not the power themselves. Words repeated until they no longer have feeling behind them are completely impotent.

Thoughts are often more important than words. The energy of our thoughts creates an energy field all around us. This field can be filled with either harmonious or disharmonious feelings. Which translates into energy. This energy field will magnetically pull like energies right to us.

Nothing is to be feared from idle words or idle thoughts. Unless the words and/or thoughts have feeling behind them - they will not create what is thought about or spoken. The only trick is to know for sure what is prompting the thoughts or words.

One of the aspects of fear is - it's "sneaky." We may sometimes say or think things from a low level fear of which we may not be fully aware. It is advisable to watch your words and thoughts to find what feelings may be driving them. It is the energies of those feelings that will create.

In order to create your desired conditions, send positive energies into the universe. Don't concern yourself with idle thoughts or words. But - be sure you know whether a feeling energy lies behind them.

Perspective on Fear

The one thing that paralyzes more efforts at transformation than anything else - is fear. Fear stops your positive creative power in its tracks. It will create for you everything you don't want. Since fear is thrown at us from every direction, it's difficult to escape. That leaves a change of perception as the only viable option.

Learn to listen to the still, small voice within you - the one that never tries to hold you back. The one that supports you and keeps you moving forward. When others throw fear your way or try to make you doubt your decisions - trust yourself! Trust the inner voice. That voice comes from your spirit. The part of you that knows there is nothing to be feared.

It isn't necessary to deny your fear. Acknowledge it and allow it to move *through* you. You only get into trouble when you allow fear to become "stuck" within you. Fear is only a feeling - and it can be examined and re-routed, so to speak. With a change in perception, fear will be transmuted into the positive energies that create awesome transformations.

We live in a benevolent universe! In truth, there is nothing in this universe to fear except what we create ourselves. When you decide to become One with the true harmony of the universe - rather than in your own fears - all the energies of the universe will move to assist you. You then become a co-participant in the wonder of creation.

We were never intended to live filled with fear - to allow it to make us ill - or drive us into death. That isn't the plan of the universal spirit. That's our plan - and we can always change our minds.

When you decide you don't wish to live in fear anymore, you will be given the strength to face whatever it is that you fear. As always - it's your decision.

These thoughts on fear are paraphrased from one of my favorite books, "I Come as a Brother," by Bartholomew. I know them to be true through my own experience! I recommend this book!

Still, Small Voice

Nearly every time I mention listening to the "still, small voice" within you when you need right guidance, I can predict what will happen next. Sure enough, someone immediately tells me about the "loud, huge voice" that never keeps still. Okay - let's go with that.

Nearly everyone hears more than one voice in their head. The question seems to be which one to follow when choosing a path. Bear in mind, the still, small voice I mentioned comes from your inner spirit.

The "loud, huge voice" comes from an entirely different place. Listen carefully and you may even recognize it. It's the sound of "tapes" from the past.

This is the voice that says, "You're not good enough to get it!" when you apply for a promotion. When you look in the mirror, it's the voice you hear saying, "No one will ever love you because you're too short / tall / fat / thin / dumb / smart." And, it's the voice you hear telling you that you don't deserve to have your dreams come true. It is also the voice that will convince you to do something the still, small voice knows is wrong for you.

Forget that voice! It's nothing more than someone's opinion of you at some point in time. It doesn't need to be your opinion. You hear the huge, loud voice more clearly because it's habitual. You're used to it. You know what it will say before you hear it.

Granted the still, small voice is usually harder to hear. Your spirit is quiet - it has no need to yell. This is the part of you that knows who you are. It knows you are a unique creation. And, it knows you deserve all good things.

If you need help learning to hear the still, small voice - go back to the Appendix (which you should have read first) and re-read the chapter entitled, "Meditation Made Easy." It is exactly what it says - easy. At first you'll only hear the still, small voice in the silence. You must discover how to become truly silent - and it isn't nearly as tough as you think it is!

The still, small voice only seems that way compared to the other. Give it as much attention as you do the huge, loud voice and it will grow stronger every day.

Basic Creation

Before we go into the individual processes for creating money, health and relationships, we need to know the general techniques that work in all areas. These techniques should be used no matter what you are creating.

I can't say this too many times - be *sure* to read through the techniques in *all* life areas. You will find examples of things in each that will help in all the others.

After the chapters on specific life areas, you will find a checklist to be used after you finish the process - while you wait for your creation to appear. Following that, are some additional tips that may need to be taken into consideration.

General Tips for Creating

Be Bold

Remember: *you deserve all good things!* Decide to be BOLD. Get exactly what you want. Don't wimp out thinking you "can't" get something - or you "don't deserve it."

Remember, the universe will only send you what you can - or will - accept. Decide now to be willing to accept *all* good things. Think BIG - create BIG - decide you *deserve* the very *best* of everything!

Image with Power

The imaging process may be one of the most important. You must see what you want in your mind whether it is wealth - health - or love.

Imagine everything in colorful detail. Envision every detail right down to the color of your shoes. Create every single aspect of your image. Involve yourself totally.

To give the image the most power you will need to use *all* of your physical senses. Imagine the sounds, scents, touch feelings and, if possible, the tastes involved in your visualization. Using all the senses is what helps you develop the feelings needed to create. *Being there* is what gives the image its power.

The unconscious mind "sees" these images clearly since they are based on the feelings you generate with the image. The unconscious mind cannot differentiate between what it sees in your imagination and what it sees in the outer world. It accepts it all as true - without question. Then, it begins moving you in the direction needed to fulfill the truth of those feelings. *So, be very clear in your imaging and inject it with powerful feelings.*

Signs of Land

Go back to Part One of *The MASTER COURSE* and re-read the chapter entitled, "Signs of Land." This step should be used in all creative processes at the point where you are to put it out of your mind and expect your result.

Each "sign of land" is evidence your creation is on its way to you. By recognizing - and giving thanks for - each "sign of land," (no matter how small) you are reinforcing you know your creation is on its way. Remember - gratitude is a huge magnet for good.

Pay attention! Refusing to see those first "signs of land" may keep you from recognizing something you need to see. Appreciating and giving thanks for each one of them will keep expanding the energies!

Setting Dates

It is sometimes helpful to set a date when you want something accomplished. This is something you'll need to decide for yourself.

If you set a date, then worry about whether you will receive your creation by that date - it's counterproductive. However, as you get better and better at creating your life, you'll gain the confidence that you *can* set a date.

Sometimes, dates are set for us. Perhaps you need money by a certain date for a particular situation. Or, you find you'll have to move to a new residence and have to vacate your old one by a certain date. You need the money - or the perfect place to live - on a time schedule.

In these instances, you can feel perfectly safe expecting your creation to manifest by a certain date. You know it has to be there on time - and it will be. It's all part of the intent and commitment.

Common Sense

Even with processes, sometimes we have to use some common sense along with them. We also need to *take the next right step*.

Several years ago, I heard a minister turned stand-up comic. Most of his material was in really bad taste but nearly all of it contained a germ of truth. He had a real knack for seeing the nonsense in the human condition.

He talked about the starving people in Ethiopia. He said, instead of sending them food, we should be sending them U-Haul trucks - so they could get the hell out of the desert! That, of course they were starving - and always would - as long as they lived in the desert!

Now, that may sound a mean. But, there was that germ of truth!

Back in the 1980s, most of the oil fields in Texas were shut down. What did most of the oil workers do? They went to California and worked in the oil fields there. They got the hell out of the desert!

My point is ... when you release the energies for what you want to materialize into the universe, then, you need to look around and see what you need to do. If you need to get out of the desert - *do it!*

Create Without Harm

I want to give you one caution if you are creating money. You might want to affirm you will receive it without bringing harm to anyone else.

Universal law works. And, it isn't always very particular how it works. I know more than one person has created money that actually came through an inheritance when it came.

You don't want to outline where something has to come from. But, you might want to qualify that one point. "Without harm to anyone else."

Cast the Burden

When we come to the "Forget it" step of the creative process, we need to alert the universe it will be receiving the energy to transform into our creation. If we feel the need to create something for our lives, this indicates we are living with the burden of lack in some area.

We alert the universe we are relieving ourselves of that burden by "casting the burden" onto the universe for resolution. This amounts to "letting go" of all the fear and handing it over to a greater power to bring us what we need. Be sure to thank the universe in advance for removing this burden! Then - know it is done!

"Casting the burden" is a critical part of the creative process! But, don't become confused here. You are a part of that greater power. *You are one with that greater power!* We "cast the burden" onto the wholeness of that power in order to get our own unconscious fears out of the picture. This is also known as surrender!

Creating Wealth

Before we begin the actual process of creating financial security, let's discuss a bit more something I mentioned back in Part One of the Course. I referred to it as, "deprivation-consciousness." Another word for this insidious condition is "poverty-consciousness."

Before you begin the techniques to create wealth, you'll need to be sure you aren't being counter-productive by exhibiting signs of poverty-consciousness. It's difficult to list them since they are different with different people. However, you can look for these types of behavior.

Anything you do done from a place of apparent lack is showing this poverty-consciousness. If you try to use positive techniques at the same time you are continuing to wallow in poverty, the universe will create where the greatest feeling lies. And, that's always in the emotion of fear that there won't be enough.

Look for behaviors like the following - or anything similar:

Do you save the "good things" for some special occasion that may never happen? Don't. Use them every day until your unconscious mind understands you expect to have these kinds of things to use as a matter of course. Save them and all that will happen is your heirs will enjoy them.

Do you routinely go to "All You Can Eat" restaurants? If this is a habit, chances are it's coming from a need to get the most for your money out of fear of there not being enough. If you go because you're very hungry tonight, and you like their food - that's fine. But, if you go out of some sense of needing to get "more" - it's probably brought about by an inner fear of starvation. That's a pretty strong fear!

Chances are you won't eat any more than you'd get at a regular restaurant anyway. If you can eat enough to get more than your money's worth, you're probably overweight and should be reading the chapters on health.

Do you feel yourself getting angry inside if you're asked to donate to something? Let it go. That's a fear-of-lack feeling. Give what you can comfortably give and thank the universe you have it give. Send it along with the love energy to go out and multiply. It will.

Do you find yourself needing to use everything up completely? The loaf of bread is stale but you won't buy another until it's gone? Or, you turn the bottle of dishwashing detergent upside down to get the last drop out of it? Or, you take those little tiny bits of soap - put them in a nylon bag - and use them for something else? All those activities are fear-of-lack behavior.

You will need to be extremely watchful of yourself to recognize all the things you do out of fear of there not being enough. In fact, sometimes this isn't conscious - it's old habits. But it sends the universe the same message.

Some fear of lack behaviors:

- Needing to use everything completely

- Saving things - especially if they've already been used

- Saving things because you "might" use them someday

- Needing to eat everything on the plate

- Only shopping in discount or thrift stores

- Using valuable time to find the gas station where you save 2¢ a gallon

- Using or wearing things that are irreparably ragged, torn or stained

- Refusing to buy even small things that would make your life easier

- Always buying products of lesser quality because they're less expensive

- Not taking care of what you do have

- Allowing yourself to "look" poor

These are only a few and do not include things you do to help the ecology of the Earth such as using both sides of paper. Provided that's the real reason you do it. As always - it's all in the intent. Why are you doing that? You'll need to be ruthlessly honest with yourself. You can't fool the unconscious mind.

And, of course, you'll need to watch your words - constantly! Don't entertain your friends and family with stories of how poor you are - or how you got "ripped off" or can't afford something. You're bound to get a lot of feelings involved and make the entire situation worse.

Take Action:

Take a few days and watch yourself. Examine everything you do and look at why you do it. Don't make excuses – you know the bottom line. If it's something coming from poverty-consciousness – do something different!

During those same days, pay attention to everything coming out of your mouth. If you hear something that makes you "sound" poor – you'll know to change the way you say it next time.

For instance, instead of saying, "I can't afford it," - teach yourself to say, "I don't choose to spend money on that right now." It's true - and you're replacing a negative with a positive. You're also back in control!

A sure sign of poverty consciousness is saving everything. Using things beyond their intended use or allowing things to be run down in general just shows the universe you don't expect anything more.

This causes stagnated energy around you - snuffing out any possibility new things can come to you. Of course they can't! There's no place to put them! All that blocked energy will get you nowhere fast down the road to prosperity.

In order to come out of poverty-consciousness, you'll need to be willing to release everything - including the past. It doesn't matter what you didn't have yesterday - yesterday is gone. And, I promise you - the children in China will not starve *because you* didn't "clean up your plate!"

Today can be the beginning of a whole new life. It's your choice. If you allow fear to stand in your way, you'll only choose by default.

Steps to Creation

Before you begin this process, go back and re-read the chapter on "Commitment" in Part Two. I can't tell you how important it is you understand this thoroughly.

Without commitment - nothing happens. You won't be able to get into the full feelings of expectation necessary for creating your desires. You must fully *intend to have* whatever it is you want.

Once you are fully committed - and your intention is clear - your success is assured. This is when things begin to happen which will completely surprise you. This is when the universe knows exactly what to do.

Choose It

Now you're ready to begin bringing things into your life. From earlier chapters, you have decided exactly what you want. You've removed anything that might be standing in its place - and you've banished any idea you can't have it.

We have seven major steps in this process. You have, hopefully, completed the first two - which are to create a vacuum for the universe to fill - and *choose!* And, I trust you have chosen carefully!

This 7-step process works no matter what you wish to create. Money - wellness - a loving relationship - it's all the same.

Image It

The next step is to image. We need to get a very clear picture of what we want and we have several different ways to do this.

First, visualize it. See it in your mind in vivid detail. Involve all of your physical senses in this and always put yourself in the picture.

If it's a new car you want, see yourself driving it. Smell the "new car" fragrance - hear the motor purring - feel the grain of the leather seats or your hands on the steering wheel.

Move around in the picture. See yourself doing whatever you would be doing in the situation where you have what you want. Then, surround this entire mental picture with light! Remember - light is energy.

This is not a daydream!

Most of us have had many, many daydreams that never happened. So, we know just seeing something in the mind doesn't always bring it into our lives. This goes back to what we believe. When we daydream, we nearly always call it what it is. A fantasy.

We never really believe it's going to happen. We're just playing games. It's like idle words - no power. Idle thoughts have no power either. If they did, we'd all be driving around in great big limousines!

And, we'd all be up to our necks in real, live dragons, or something. Children are people too. Look at all the things they visualize that don't show up in the living room. But, children also know they're just playing.

The difference we want here is to invoke both feeling and belief into the situation. Know it can be yours and inject all the joy you will feel when you receive it into the image! Remember - everything works both ways. If the new job brings you happiness - then happiness over knowing you'll find the new job can bring you the job.

Right here might be a good place to remind you not to be so specific you limit your possibilities. Don't decide you must have a certain kind of car - a particular job - a certain amount of money - or anything that specific. To do so is to limit the universe. Don't. Given the chance, the universe is very likely to send you much more than you could ever have hoped for.

You can also image by writing - and this is *very powerful*. As you're writing, you'll have feelings about this thing you wish to manifest. Now remember - the words on paper do not create. The feelings you have about them do.

As you're writing, you'll begin to own this thing you want. It's all right there - in your own handwriting. It's part of you. You begin to become one with it. If you want it - *you must become one with it*. You must see it as yours!

Remember, all feelings come from a basis of either love or fear. As you visualize and write - *you must incorporate loving feelings.* And, all happy feelings are loving feelings!

Claim It

Now, you've chosen. You're sure of what you want. You're sure you know it's possible for you. And, you've imaged. You've pictured it and written it down. You have involved feelings, giving power to thought.

Next, we use words as the vehicle to move our creative energies out into the universe. We're going to use the spoken word and we're going to call our creation forth. We don't hope for it! We don't ask for it! We affirm we already have it.

The best way to do this is simply to give thanks it is yours. That it is already yours. You become One with it.

We don't say, "I want ..." or even, "I have ..." It's, "Thank you that I AM prosperous." Use the words, "I AM ..." to become One with it! Those two words are the creation. *We always become what we say we are!*

Let's stop right here and think about that for a minute. This is so important!

How many times have you said, "I'm (I AM) always broke" - "I'm (I AM) scared" - "I'm (I AM) sick." The instant you say "I AM," you fully embrace whatever you just named. You become One with it! And you feel even more broke - more scared - more ill. You instantly become the thing you say you are!

Use the words, "I AM" correctly!

It's helpful to consider you couldn't - or wouldn't - have the desire if the creation weren't possible for you. So why haven't you already manifested it? Because you simply haven't accepted it yet. With your words, you will accept it by giving thanks for it.

You can find hundreds of books with thousands of affirmations in them if you want to use them. I never touch them. If an affirmation comes from your heart - in your own words - it's full of personal feeling. And, feeling is what we want to put out there. Use your personal affirmation to establish your word. This is the very best way to charge your affirmations with feeling!

Just be careful not to continue to parrot the words until they lose their meaning. In truth - you only need to make the statement once!

Name it - claim it - and love it. Don't try to do this without emotion. Love is the causal energy that will bring you what you want. Just as fear is the causal energy that brings you what you don't want!

Act As If...

So now, we have: *create a void - choose - image - write - call forth*. Then what? At this point, you have two choices.

The first is to, "act as if" the thing you wish to manifest is already yours. Further along this path, that's exactly what you'll do. But, when you're just beginning to use this consciousness that can be pretty dangerous.

If you call forth money to pay the bills the first of the month - then, "act as if" by sitting down and just writing and mailing off checks - do you want to explain this to the gas company when their check bounces? "Oh well, I was just creating money and I had to act as if I already had it." They'll tell you to act as if you had heat!

You know, the whole time you're writing those checks, you're going to be thinking about how the money isn't really there. That's going to scare you - and lo and behold - we have a feeling that creates an empty bank account.

Or, you could "act as if" by going out and buying some little thing that makes you feel rich. Okay. But, even doing that, we know it's really just a game. You've got to give yourself credit for some intelligence here. Don't play games with the universe. It isn't necessary and you don't have to.

There are some small ways to it. You can get ready. Go pick out your new car saying, "This, or something better." Take a picture of it home and hang it on your refrigerator or someplace where you'll see it often. It works even better to hang it on a plant. There it picks up the growth energy - an influence of Feng Shui. Your creation begins to grow!

You can make room for what it is you want. You can expect it.

But, to my way of thinking, this comes under a little different heading called "commitment." Once you *fully commit* to having something, things will begin to happen you could never have imagined. Help will seem to come out of thin air.

Forget It

Remember, I said you have two choices when it comes to the sixth step in the creative process. The first choice is to, "Act as if ..." Personally, I prefer the second since the first can seem so much like game-playing. The second option is to *forget it!*

I think this is the better - and much faster - way. Choose it - image it - call it forth - and forget it! Drop it. Know it is established and get out of the way! Don't keep looking for it, other than to recognize "signs of land.". Because, until it comes, every time you don't see it, it reinforces the apparent lack. Just take the next right step you can take toward the arrival of what you want - and wait. You won't have to wait too long.

Make the commitment and the universe moves. You don't have to play any games. If what you are creating crosses your mind - and it will - just say (out loud), "Thank you." Know you thought of it because it is on its way to you.

When you do this, you're releasing the energies into the universe where they can do their work. As long as you're playing games with it - you haven't let it go. At some point, we must let it go.

It works even better to do this just before falling asleep. Not because you are training the sub-conscious. Things don't come *from* the sub-conscious. They come *through* that creative channel. It's an energy source - not an intelligence. When you go directly to sleep, you completely release those energies into the universe through that channel.

Give What You Want To Receive

Now, there's one more thing. It's the seventh, and last, step - and it's very important. *You must give what you want to receive* - on a daily basis!

If you want money - give money! You'll no more run out of money than you'll run out of love - as long as you keep circulating it. You will only run out if you're afraid you will! Keep everything good circulating. What goes out must come back! It probably won't come back from the same place you gave it but - it will come back! It's the *Law!*

In some places you'll hear you must tithe to a church in order to receive prosperity. In truth, whatever you give - freely and lovingly - counts. You can give a few bucks to a homeless person. It counts. You can give to a children's hospital. It counts. You can give (not loan) to a friend in need. It counts.

If you want new clothes - give away some of the ones you want replaced. Don't sell them - give them! If you want to perk up your whole house with new things, sure it's okay to have a yard sale. But, give away a few things during the course of the sale.

The only trick is: *it must be given freely and lovingly*. After you do it for a while, you'll begin to lose the fear and begin to feel good about yourself for doing it. Now you've created the positive love energies. And, you'll find it doesn't hurt a bit!

Creating Health & Anti-Aging

All of the steps in the process for creating financial security can also be used to create perfect health. I'll tell you how to do this in detail more specific to health issues. But, we have other things we need to consider when dealing with our physical well-being too.

As mentioned in former Parts of this course, stress is the number one reason we have ill health at all. Stress can be found at the bottom of nearly all disease - and accidents too. Unfortunately, we can never eliminate stress. What we can do is learn to live with it so it doesn't kill us.

The very best thing you can do to begin this process is to get into the habit of using the meditation technique mentioned in the Appendix of *The MASTER COURSE*. If you are having health problems, try to use it twice a day for 20 minutes each time.

It's also helpful to recognize stress and accept it without becoming unduly upset. You may do this by acknowledging stress is present - thank it for doing its job (which is to warn you) - and then excuse it from duty.

Do not say, "I am stressed." Do say, "I see stress is present ..." Do not become one with it by use of the words, "I AM."

The same process may be used if you suffer from chronic pain. Pain is a warning something is out of balance. You don't want to "get rid of" pain until you know why it's manifesting in your body. Then, you can lessen it, or excuse it, from your presence.

In working with your health, it's also necessary to release fear and chaotic energy. Try to realize nothing can happen to you without your permission. However, the presence of fear sends out energies bringing about all kinds of unpleasant circumstances.

The most important thing you can learn about your health was in Part Two, under, "Cell Relationships." Once you become friends with the cells of your body, and understand they will follow your direction, there's very little you can't do to take care of yourself.

As you begin to take control of the cells of your body, you will find fear is beginning to be relieved. We feel fear when we feel out of control. In truth, we are never out of control when it comes to our bodies although it often appears that way.

Maintaining youth is one of the things I've been most asked about. This is also one of the most difficult to do since it is so ingrained in us we must grow old. Although it isn't true at all that we have to show our age, it's nearly impossible for people to accept. However, we have a few things that can be done to reasonably slow down the aging process.

First - don't act your age! By this I mean, do not allow others to tell you how you should behave based on the number of years you've been on this planet. The only reason we "slow down" is because we expect - and are expected - to do so. Don't do it!

It truly is all "acting" anyway. Pay attention. How old do you feel inside? Although the body appears to age, the part of us inside - the real us - continues to feel the same as we did in our prime. We only "act" a certain way based on what's expected of us. *This is a choice!*

The second thing to do is cut out the "death talk" mentioned in Part One. This is a chapter that should be re-read until you can completely stop making all the statements telling your body to age or die. *This is extremely important!* Remember, your cells don't need your feeling behind your words. They hear the words and begin doing exactly what they hear, without any judgment or argument.

In the area of health, we have many different conditions. It isn't possible to try to cover them all in a course of this kind. In using the creative process you may have to give some concentrated thought to just how to tailor the process to your particular situation. However, no matter what it is - all the basics will apply.

Steps to Creation

As in creating wealth, we have the same steps in the creative process. This is in addition to the incredible quality of our cells to create for us. Again, I assume, in reading through the first chapters of this course, you have already chosen what you want. You have also chosen carefully, and you now understand you deserve all good things - including life and perfect health. Then, once you have mastered intent and commitment, you are ready to take the next step.

Image

Picture it. Picture your perfect body in your mind. This is especially helpful for weight control. I already covered how to do that in Part Two in regard to learning to love your body - and for controlling its size.

You may have another physical quality you would like to see gone. It may come from an accident or disease. The same mirror techniques are used in changing anything of this type.

When not using the mirror, use as many of your physical senses as you can when imaging bodily perfection. Picture yourself as you would like to be - in a setting where you might enjoy everything around you. Possibly out in nature but wherever you're most comfortable.

Smell the fresh cut grass around you - the fragrance of spring. See the clear blue sky - maybe mountains in the distance - a waterfall - anything you find pleasant. Feel the bark of a tree - the velvet of moss - the warmth of the sun - the coolness of shade. Hear a trickling stream - the birds singing - the chirp of crickets. Even taste a blade of grass.

Use all your physical senses in the visualization. This will elicit feelings of contentment - defined, "love." Doing this while visualizing yourself in perfect health sends the right energies out into the universe to create your vision for yourself. Be sure to "see" yourself well and strong - maybe doing things you can't seem to do right now.

Don't forget to surround yourself with the energy of light in your image.

Next, do the imaging in writing. Write down what is already yours. Always use positive statements and always be explicit. Again - don't ask for anything. Do not write, "I want ..." - or - "I have ..."

Be emphatic that the healing you wish is already manifest. Give thanks you already have what it is you want. Here you may be as detailed as you like. The more clearly you write it, the easier it is for the universe (and the cells of your body) to understand. Don't send mixed messages. *Be emphatic!*

If you wish to write affirmations, that may also be helpful. Try to come up with your own - some very personal to you. Choose words with plenty of feeling involved. It's your body - you are involved at the most personal level. Make your affirmations uniquely yours and write them with as much feeling as you can muster.

Use the words, "I AM ..." - such as, "I AM in perfect health" - "I AM well and strong" - "I AM youthful and full of energy." Become one with what you want. Always remember - *we become what we say we are!*

Remember - only use the love energies. You want feelings of love to go out to do your bidding.

As with building wealth, you can also use pictures in changing anything about your body. A photo of yourself doing something you believe you can't do now - placed where you will see it often - is a powerful message to your cells. Just remember not to look at it and think about how you can't do that anymore - or don't look like that anymore. Calmly affirm, "I AM that!"

Claim It

Next, we'll give all the feelings a vehicle with which to move out into the universe. Words make up the vehicle that carries the feelings out to create.

You may wish to use your affirmations here too. Just don't allow them to become repetitive and lose their meaning. In claiming perfect health, I think it's far better to use words to simply talk to the cells of your body.

By now, I hope you have established communication with your cells. You need to have a relationship with them - a good one. You need to send them love - thank them for the job they do for you - and give them loving direction. Remember - don't ask. *Tell* them what to do and expect them to do it. And, don't watch to see if they're doing it. They will. Maybe quicker than you think.

I once woke up in the night, around 3 AM, with what appeared to be a horrible head cold. My head was completely "stuffed up" and I couldn't even breathe through my nose. My head hurt and felt huge. I also appeared to be running a slight fever - with chills - although I didn't check.

I sat on the edge of my bed and had a talk with my cells. I thanked them for alerting me to the fact that I - once again - needed to slow down.

I also reminded them I had important things to do the next day and I did not have time to be ill, but I would rest a bit after I finished. I told them I was going back to sleep and I expected them to right things by morning.

The next morning, when I woke at 6 AM, my head was clear as a bell and I felt fine. In just three hours my body had returned to complete normality.

Act As If ...

As mentioned in the wealth section, I am not a great fan of "acting as if." However, it seems to work for some people so I will offer it here for your consideration.

In matters of health, it does make a bit more sense to me. We can act differently. We can choose to ignore how "old" we're supposed to act and act the age we feel inside. We can stop saying we're "too tired," and get back into life. We can even stop allowing others to treat us as if we're "over the hill." *Stop giving them permission!*

If we are ill, we can stop complaining. We may not be able to do everything we'd like to right then, but we can stop calling it to attention. We can try harder. We can intend to get better and start moving into actions showing even a small amount of recovery.

Even depression can be treated by "acting as if." Acting happy - even when we aren't - has a marvelous recuperative affect. It's a "do it anyway" type of thing. Sure, it can be very hard to get started. But, it's not impossible. It can be done!

The endorphins produced by laughter have the effect of lessening the depression. So, acting as if we're happy - even when we aren't - can bring about the production of the needed neurotransmitters that make us feel happy in reality.

Now don't confuse this with "stuffing" bad feelings. It isn't. The feelings of depression aren't denied - we are simply making another choice about how we want to feel. When we're feeling better, the issues that brought on the depression are much easier to deal with.

And ... Stop Planning to Die!

You've heard it a bazillion times. "You're only as old as you feel." "Age is just a state of mind." But, how many people really believe it? Not many.

Youth and vitality are a major concern on the planet today. I'm glad to see it. Maybe - finally - we're getting the picture that growing "old" isn't all that necessary. Age is more a matter of how we "act" than anything else.

From the day we're born we're told how old to act. "Grow up." "You're too old to cry." Later, it's, "Don't act like a child." "People your age shouldn't dress like that." And the one I really love - "Act your age!" Whatever that means. Truth is - we "act" our way into old age - and then right into the grave.

I have explained how the cells of our bodies do our exact bidding. They take orders - whether we give those orders consciously or unconsciously. They follow our exact directions. Let your belief system tell them to grow old and that's exactly what they'll do. Remember - you always act on your beliefs!

Think of all the ways you direct your body to grow old rather than to maintain youth and vitality. It doesn't have to be spoken. Do you already have your burial plot? Think your body cells weren't with you when you bought it? Do you think they didn't get the message? That very action told them what you expect of them.

"To act," indicates playing a role. As the number of years you've been on this planet increase - and you "act" like it - you are simply playing the role that's been assigned. *You* are the director of the drama of your life even though you play the starring role. As the director, you can decide to act differently. Trust me - the cells of your body will fall right into the new role.

Start "acting" like you intend to live and thrive. Grow in wisdom rather than age. Every action you take that indicates growing old is a message that will be carried out by the cells of your body. Act as if you are "youthing" rather than aging!

Forget It

If you don't choose to "act as if" - or, for some reason that isn't possible, you can use the alternative fourth step. Forget it. Choose - visualize - name it - claim it - then forget it.

I gave a good example of this in Part One, in the chapter, "Health, Youth & Physical Well-being." When I was dealing with a torn retina, I didn't have time to worry about it. I directed my cells to repair the damage - *emphatically* - and then I forgot about it and expected them to do their work. They did. The same way they got rid of that head cold while I went back to sleep.

Any time we create anything to perfection, we aren't thinking about it consciously all the time. We state (in one way or another) what we expect - then we expect exactly that and wait for it to happen. This is exactly how we create everything we don't want! Expectation has a very strong, drawing magnetism!

Everything works both ways! If we do whatever we know how to do using the creative processes - then forget it - the same thing happens. We're out of the way and the universe does its work.

In the case of health and aging, it's possible to use both "act as if" and "forget it" at the same time. We can make a decision to act differently - then do it. At the same time, we can stop thinking and worrying about the issue we want healed and turn our attention to more positive things. It's the best of all possible worlds!

Give What You Want To Receive

And, finally, don't forget to give what you want to receive. How can you do that? It's fairly easy ... You want good health - help someone else have better health. Volunteer - help others - give loving support to someone else who is ill - you can always find someone who is worse off than you. And, don't even think about playing the "I know how you feel," game. Do not mention your own situation. Do not give it any attention at all!

Helping someone who is worse off than you has the added benefit of raising your own gratitude quotient! *Gratitude for what is already yours is mandatory!*

Creating Your Relationship

Relationships can be the hardest - or the easiest - thing to create. It has less to do with processes and more to do with what is going on inside you.

We are constantly sending out energies, based on our own experiences and beliefs about intimate love. Those energies go forth and connect with the energies of another person who has the *complementary* energy. Someone who fits our perception of what love should be.

If we are putting out negative energies, we'll go into negative types of relationships. This is hardly what you would consciously create for yourself.

So, before thinking about creating a relationship, you may need to deal with your "issues" about it. Everyone seems to have issues. There can be abandonment issues – co-dependency issues - self-esteem issues - hostility issues. We have issues ad infinitum and ad nauseam! Even my dog has issues! We love our issues. We fly them like a flag that others should stand up and salute. So I have a few words for you about issues ...

Get over them!

Look closely at your issues and you'll find every single one of them based in fear. Hang on to your issues for dear life and you'll find yourself constantly surrounded with fear energy. And what does fear create? Let's say it together:

"Fear creates what we do not want!"

How many times have you heard it? Whatever you give your attention to - increases. Hang on to those issues and you hang onto fear. Pay attention to them by constantly whining about them - and they'll grow and grow. The issues become unrecognizable as time passes and the story grows more and more dramatic. As the drama increases - so does the fear. Until finally, you'll find yourself paralyzed by it.

I've seen people go to therapy for years to deal with issues - and never get any better. Why? Because they loved their issues! Those issues gave their lives meaning. It was negative meaning - but meaning nevertheless. And, it was meaning they chose!

I've also seen people go to for short periods of time and have near miraculous recoveries. Why? Because they listened to themselves - and they wore themselves out. Just as we wear out everyone we complain to. They got tired of it - saw how it was wearing away their own life force - and decided to get over it!

That's what it takes. We get over our issues when we get tired enough of them. When we decide we're had enough of the havoc they create in our life - and in the lives of others. We get over our issues when we realize it isn't the issue that's causing the pain. The pain is caused from clinging to the issue.

Yes - it is that simple.

For as long as you cling to your "issues," you will be unable to create the joyous life you so deserve. Issues will create fear - wear you out - and create more of the very thing you fear.

Release the past. Forgive. *You must forgive!* If you have had unhappy relationships in the past, take what you can learn from them and let go of the rest. They were just learning experiences in what you don't want.

Defeat is the greatest teacher of all. You deserve to have a holy relationship! Create it!

You may also need to do some work if you have come from a dysfunctional family. You may be carrying unconscious belief systems that keep you from finding true happiness. Again - this is a place to use *The MASTER COURSE* Workbook, *"Who's Driving Your Bus?"*

In any event - whether you use the self-analysis guide, or not - you will need to go through a forgiveness process over family issues. Love is love. You need to be able to express it everywhere. Where there is unforgiveness, there is fear. Fear must be banished as much as possible before you will ever have a truly and wholly loving relationship.

In order to create a truly loving relationship, we must first be a truly loving person. That's the energy we want to send out to attract another truly loving person. This was discussed in Part Two of the Course. Go back and review the notes you made in the chapter entitled, "Intimate Relationships."

You did do the "Action Steps," didn't you? If not - do them now. *Before* you attempt to create a holy relationship.

Steps To Creation

If you have done all the work in the previous chapters of *The MASTER COURSE,* by now you should have been able to choose exactly what you wish to have in a relationship. You should know exactly what qualities you wish to find in the other person involved. Do *not* attempt to create a relationship until you are *sure* you know exactly what you want. *Choose!* Don't allow this to be chosen for you.

Let me remind you once again ... It is extremely dangerous to set your sights on a particular person. Again - what you want is not the person - it is the relationship you see yourself having with that person. A particular person may not be capable of having that type of relationship with you. Don't limit the universe!

If you're sure you want a partner and you have made a firm commitment - you have set your intent - you're ready to start!

Image

You may have already started the imaging process while you were writing down the qualities you wish to have in a mate. This is another place where you don't want to put too much emphasis on a particular area.

Your choice of physical characteristics should be watched carefully. Must your relationship be with a blonde - brown eyes - a certain height and weight? If so, go for it. But, you may be missing out on a tremendous loving relationship with a brunette.

On the other hand, there may be certain physical characteristics you simply can't tolerate. If this is the case, by all means exclude those from your mental picture.

As you image yourself with your created partner, cover all the bases. Image the two of you in different surroundings. If you like football and you want someone to share that with you, see the two of you at a football game. If you like to take walks, do the same. You need to include some of the activities you enjoy. I say "some" because you may not share every activity in your relationship. People need time away from each other too.

If your intention is to create a long-term, living together relationship - picture yourself in your home together. This is very important! One of the elements needed for a successful relationship is shared values.

Usually, values aren't something that can be changed - or that will change. What are your standards of living? Are you willing to change that? Are you able to change that? If not, be sure to picture the two of you interacting in the kind of home you want.

Picture everything. Are there children involved? Are there pets involved? What kind? Do you have a need to be in a certain city - or in the country? Place it all in the picture. In this case, it's best to leave very little to chance.

You may also image with pictures. A picture of a loving couple on the refrigerator - or hung on a plant. Preferably, one person of the couple will look similar to you. Pictures of a wedding, if that's what you want. A cruise on the Love Boat - a couple riding horseback - whatever it is you want to do.

Be sure to project yourself into the pictures every time you look at them. You must become one with those images!

Then, write it all down. Just the way you want it. You may change your list from time to time. You may add things as they occur to you or decide something isn't so important after all - and that's okay. Keep working on it!

As you write and visualize, be sure to put plenty of love into it. Feel the feelings you want to feel with your partner. Create all the feelings you want to share just as if that person were already sharing the relationship with you. Own the relationship! This is what it takes to bring it into existence. Love.

Claim It

Now begin using the words that will carry the feelings out into the universe to attract your perfect partner to you. As always, if you use affirmations, make them very personal to you. "I AM loved" and "I AM loving," are good places to start. "I AM living with my perfect partner." Remember the, "I AM."

Another little trick to use here is to tell the future partner - out loud - that you love him or her now. Say the words, "I love you," with all the feeling you can muster. In truth, you do already love this person. You just may not have met them yet. Tell them! They do exist and they will get the message. All that love will help pull them to you.

Also remember to give thanks that the perfect partner is in your life. Gratitude can't be beat for creative power! Without the words, it will take the feelings of love much longer to be carried forth to create.

Act As If ...

Creating relationships is one place where it is very appropriate to act as if you already have what it is you want. Now obviously, this doesn't mean you lock yourself away, refusing to be around others. You'll never meet your partner that way.

What you can do is get ready. Prepare your home so it's the way you want to bring your partner into it. Dress up for this new partner. Feel good about yourself. Take care of yourself! Of course, you should be doing that for yourself anyway but, in truth, many people don't. Take yourself out to dinner. Find the places you will want to share with someone else.

You can also make space for this new person in your life. Do you need to spend less time with the guys or girlfriends? Do you need to clean up your mess? You can make some closet space - or drawer space. Make a place for them to fill with their own things. You can even set the table for two! Create a space for the universe to fill.

Forget It

It may seem difficult to forget you have stated your intention to have a partner if you are "acting as if …" Not true. What you forget is you are now alone.

You forget it by knowing this partner is on the way to you. You forget it by getting ready. You forget it by not looking for this person to appear. You don't want to wonder if every person you look at is "The One." Most likely, "The One" will turn up at the time, and in the place, you least expect it anyway.

You have to turn those love energies loose into the universe for them to do their work! If you are constantly looking for your perfect partner, he or she will never arrive. Let it go. Forget it.

Give What You Want To Receive

Instead, start thinking about giving what you want to receive. Hug people - do random acts of kindness - use "Love" stamps - say something nice to everyone you meet - encourage and support others - smile at strangers! Tell people you love them. Don't withhold! Like everything else - in order to get love, *you must give love.*

Waiting For Your Creation

When you arrive at the "Forget it" step in the creative process in any area of life, you are basically finished. However, you still have some things to do that will hasten the manifestation.

- "Cast the Burden" onto the universe

- Maintain a mind-set of constant gratitude

- Maintain awareness of the universe working to bring you all good things

- Continue to "act as if ..." if that is appropriate

- Prepare your environment to receive what is on its way

- Remain undisturbed even if it "appears" your creation isn't manifesting

- Know it simply hasn't manifested yet

- Refuse to allow yourself to sink back into fear feelings

- Pay attention

- Watch for "signs of land" and give thanks for each one - no matter how small

- Stay out of the way - let the universe do its job

- Remember, "How?" is none of your business

Additional Tips

Balance is the Goal

In times such as we've been experiencing recently on the planet, it's easy to question the inherent goodness of the universe. We can't see the "good" in the devastation of death and violence resulting from wars or local tragedies. During these times, it almost seems blasphemy to claim "all things work for good." To do so would seem like denial.

Demanding answers to the "Why?" question in order to place blame is counterproductive. It only becomes productive if the information is actually used to implement change.

We live on a planet of polarity - a planet of opposites. Up/down - right/left - in/out - and seeming good/evil. In the higher consciousness, these opposites don't exist. We have created them for our own learning. Even North and South are named merely for our perceptional direction. However, they do contain different energies. As do what we call "good" and "evil."

Consider a straight line. At one end of the line, place "good." At the other end, place "evil." Walk the line - whichever way you please. At either end, you can fall off. Much "evil" has been done in the name of "good." This is the question we've been given to solve. We must find the solution that brings balance.

Now, go back to your straight line. Take the two ends of the line and bring them together to form a circle. In so doing, you have effectively eliminated the two opposites of "good" and "evil." You have brought them together to form a whole. You have brought them into balance. You have neutralized both ends of the spectrum. You have created harmony. This can only be done without judgment of any kind. It isn't easy - but it's necessary!

52 Pick-Up

Ever play 52 Pick-Up? Here's how it goes:

Two kids (usually siblings) are playing cards. They're playing by the rules of the game. One kid begins winning too often and gets pretty cocky about it. Finally, the other kid remarks, "Let's play 52 Pick-Up. I'll deal," - throws all the cards in the air - and walks out of the room saying, "Now you pick 'em up!"

No? You didn't have a bratty little sibling? No problem. The universe will be glad to fill in and play 52 Pick-Up with you. The universe deals.

Every once in a while, we receive some type of universal energies on this planet that throws all the cards in the air. You'll notice it in your own life - in the lives of people around you - as well as on a planetary scale - all at the same time.

People don't do what they're expected to do - or what they said they would do. Situations don't resolve as intended. Everything you thought you knew flies out the window. Mechanical things malfunction and technical problems abound. The expected doesn't happen - the unexpected does. Recoveries are not made. Tempers fly. Ugly surprises pop up out of nowhere. You're handed things to deal with that you don't want. Natural disasters are frequent. Wars escalate. Worst of all - if you force the issue to get something you do want - you'll live to regret it.

Not to worry.

You've heard, "Chaos comes before order?" It's a universal law. When things need to change for the greater good of the big picture, chaos ensues. You may not like it, but you have to pick up those cards before Mom gets home. The universe will provide the energies for chaos. You get to bring about order. Choose carefully - and prepare for change.

Just pick up the cards. Don't start any new games. Know you're not being singled out. Make decisions - but don't move on them. Chances are, you'll have another choice before it's over.

When the universe throws your cards in the air - look around. If you see chaos in abundance all over the planet, relax. Sit tight and just do the next right thing until the energies pass. Then - move forward into order.

Is it a Problem - or a Challenge?

Whenever I mention that when you look around and see an increase of chaos in the world - it is not a good time to start new projects, I get the same question. I'll answer it here...

The Question:

"What if I'm forced to take a new direction anyway due to circumstances beyond my control?"

The Answer:

Ah, yes, it happens. In fact, it may happen with increased frequency while the chaotic energies are on the scene. Sometimes, we do appear to be completely without choice in a matter. Problems abound. A change of perception is in order.

I hear many "positive thinkers" refuse to call a problem what it is. They prefer to use the word, "challenge." They never have problems - they only have challenges. Yikes! Look it up. Let's ask Webster.

A problem is defined as a "question proposed for solution."

A challenge is defined as a "dare, threat, or invitation to competition."

When the universe takes over and seems to force directional changes, do you want to see it as a threat - or an invitation to competition? Do you want to compete against the universe?

Your unconscious mind knows the meanings of these words. When the universe presents you with a problem to be solved - you have not been challenged to a dual! Why tell your unconscious mind you have?

Let me assure you - you never have to compete with the universe! Accept the problems you are presented as what they are. Problems! They are situations (questions) presented to you for solution. Work them out. Work through them.

If you've been suckered into viewing your problems as challenges to be overcome - stop the contest. Why try to overcome what you can solve? Why view the universe as an adversary when you can work as a team? Would you rather work something out? Or, have to overcome it?

If you have a choice during chaotic periods - lie low. If you feel forced to take a new direction due to circumstances beyond your control, see it for what it is. An opportunity to solve a problem presented for your learning.

When 2 + 2 seems to equal 5 - there's a fundamental flaw in the principle of the equation. Since the only way out is through - work through it. Find the lesson to be learned and work it out.

Expect Miracles

First, let's define what a miracle is. A miracle is a mythical concept built around magical thinking. Miracles - in the way they are generally understood - do not exist.

Now, before you accuse me of trying to wipe out one of your most cherished concepts, let me explain. Remember the words of the great philosopher, Augustine (354-430 A.D.),

> *"Miracles are not contrary to nature but only contrary to what we know about nature."*

In other words, "miracles" are simply the natural order of things!

Why then should you "expect miracles?" Because, when you are creating the circumstances of your life, your expectations determine the outcome. Expect failure and that's exactly what you will get. Expect "miracles" and that is exactly what you will manifest. At least you'll create what you may perceive to be a miracle.

Everything in the universe is set up to grant you every good thing. All you need to do is call it forth. Often, people ask for a miracle and then they wait. The miracle comes. It comes because in the act of waiting, the one who asked - let go. In letting go, the energy of the feelings behind the petition was able to move into the universe and bring back the desired result.

When we are not receiving all the good meant for us, we are mucking up the process somehow. We are disturbing the natural order of things - most likely by our belief our desires aren't important enough to be met. The true magic of the universe is in its structure for allowing us to create whatever we desire.

> *This is the natural order of things. Call forth your desired results with feeling! Let go of the energy – and expect your "miracle."*

The Master's Path

I can't say it enough - these creative processes are based in principle - the principles I gave you in Part One of this course. Students seem to need to prove to themselves the principles work before their fears are completely removed.

You can take every step of any process I've given you - go to the list of principles in Part One - and find the principle behind each step. And, that's exactly what you should do! Figure out why they work!

Then you can begin using all the techniques interchangeably. You will begin to use them unconsciously. You will begin moving toward the Master's Path.

Would you believe me if I told you these processes aren't even necessary? Processes are steps. They are the steps by which we let go of falsity. By that, I mean - steps by which we let go of incorrect and erroneous beliefs. That's all processes are! We believe we don't have something - the process brings it to us.

They are not magical rituals for producing things we want. They simply help us get from Point A to Point B in understanding the truth available to us.

They don't help us in *doing* truth - but in *understanding* it. The truth is - we don't need the processes at all. They are steps. In the beginning, we work through these steps - one at a time - and in time, we begin to understand and know the principles behind the steps.

This means we are moving into spiritual consciousness. As we move further into that consciousness, the principles become a part of us. We accept them. We believe them. We know them!

There is a point where we acquire the insight to exactly what those principles are doing. It's, "Aha! Now I get it!" And we never, consciously, work the process again because the process is now working us.

It has become a part of us - a part of the way we function. It's the way we live our life. Unless we're talking about it, we don't have to think about it anymore. We are no longer working the process - or "working" the principles because we're *living* the process - *living the principles*. They have become our habit patterns. We don't consciously work at anything once it becomes a habit.

So these processes I give you are nothing more than steps to help you let go of the erroneous belief in lack of any kind - by teaching you to use spiritual principle. Once you completely accept spiritual principle, you never have to consciously use the processes again.

When we finally gain insight into the truth, it becomes part of us. We can't do anything but express whatever it is we've been using the process for. Why? Because we're automatically using spiritual law correctly - without thinking about it.

It would be so much easier if we would just accept the truth that all we're meant to have in our lives is absolute good. Then it would just manifest without all the processes. To think yourself there is to be there! But, we're so hard-headed, we have to set about proving it to ourselves first!

Now, I'm not trying to take your processes away from you. In fact, I hope you'll use them until you come to full realization of the principles involved. But, get on with it! Don't think they are the end of the road! We cannot reach full spiritual consciousness until we give them up!

People love their processes. They love their affirmations. They love everything that goes along with them. Of course, they do! These things give them something they didn't have before - and they'll fight to hang on to them.

Now, here's the sad part. The reason we fight to hang on to the process is we're still afraid that we can't have the things they bring us unless we use the process. Then, we're stuck in the process. We have not accepted the principle behind the process. We may accept it intellectually but we haven't fully *realized it* as part of who we are.

There is still separation from the power we are. The process is the power. The affirmation is the power. The meditation is the power. People say, "The process works - those affirmations work - meditation works."

The process doesn't work! Affirmations don't work! Meditation doesn't work!

Spirit works! *Principle* works! *The Law* works! All the rest of those things are just tools! They are tools that put principle into action - through the use of Universal Law.

But, we can use the processes until we realize that *principle is always in action* and we are not required to activate our good. All we have to do is accept it!

Yes - we only have to accept it - to know it - to fully recognize the truth and accept all good things as our birthright as a child of the universe. Then we stop dancing around and just go directly to the Light.

Then we live those laws and we don't need to concern ourselves with the process. We automatically activate the principles for absolute good by our knowledge of who we are!

At that point, we become a *Master* at what we do!

Once you start down the Master's Path, you will begin to recognize the *One Principle* - the *Principle of Oneness*. You will state it - forget it - and manifest it almost instantly. You will recognize - *you cannot be separated from your good*.

You won't ask for - or try to create anything. You will simply accept what is already yours.

For Business Owners

Everything written in *The MASTER COURSE* pertaining to financial prosperity applies to those who are involved in business. Use of the universal principles will bring you a whole new outlook on business. The Course isn't only written for people to use in their personal lives.

When you apply these principles - and use the techniques and processes given in this Course - you will soon find yourself surrounded with business associates and customers of a higher caliber. Once you learn to apply the Principle of Oneness, your business will take off in ways you couldn't have imagined.

You will lose the fear that holds any business owner back. You'll come to know you were meant to be a success in your chosen field. You will treat people differently, drawing to you those who are of like mind when it comes to ethical business practices. These are the people you can depend on - and who will come to depend on you - to get things done.

If you will use the techniques and processes offered in this Course, you'll manifest the dreams you undoubtedly had when you decided to work at your own business. You may change some of your goals as you begin to feel your right direction. Once you begin to remove some of the chaotic energy the world delivers to us daily, you'll have a clean path to success.

Those who learn and apply the universal principles come to be people who work through the heart center. This means you are always radiating the energy of love - which is the energy that creates all good things for you.

Understanding of the universal principles will cause you to stop and think. It will help you see the outcome of certain situations before you go into them. You will see why it's better to just do the next right thing in any given circumstance. When we wonder why things happen to us, it's easy to find how we created it ourselves.

The habit of giving that extra something - going that extra mile - for your customers will pay off handsomely. When it is done from this new position of working with the universe, *you'll always get back more than you gave.*

You may also find yourself willing to give a portion of what you make with your business to those less fortunate. Freely giving from the heart center will create a circulation of the energies of abundance, bringing abundance back to you - many times multiplied. You will find yourself freely giving help where you see the need. So, of course, when you need help, it will show right up on your doorstep.

None of this means you will become ineffectual in your business dealings. You can certainly remain a tough-minded businessperson. What it means is you will balance necessary "toughness" with the energies of recognized Oneness - rather than find yourself off-center from the energies of fear. It adds to your effectiveness when you can create exactly the outcome you want for any project!

Balance is the name of the game in business!

I'll share a personal story with you ...

Although I had taught *The MASTER COURSE* in seminars and workshops for several years, I had never written it down. In 1999, I decided to put it into an eBook to market online. In the process of trying to get everything set up, I managed to get myself scammed several times. I was relatively new online and had some fear and stress over "doing it right." So, of course, fear brought me a few problems to cope with.

With *The MASTER COURSE* less than 50% written, I finally lost my patience. I decided something had to be done about the way business was conducted online! The Course was put on hold while I established the International Council of Online Professionals (iCop™) – which later became Chamber of Commerce – on the Web.™ I had a vision and I went after it with a vengeance.

I became so immersed in "the fight" against unethical online business practices, I nearly forgot everything I knew about how to create success. And, this was after quite a number of years of living my life through the conscious use of universal principles. Before working online, I had even reached a place where I rarely thought about the principles - I just automatically used them.

Yet, a good dose of disharmonious energy and I seemed to forget everything I knew! I even got into the "normal" online routine of working 15 to 18 hours a day at the computer. This effectively took away even my time for practicing the Pranic Breath meditation!

I mention this because we seemed to work in a disharmonious environment online. It got me and I was considered an expert on the use of these energies! I would like for it not to trip you up as you deal with the everyday frustrations of business.

In fact, although the universe had been nagging at me for quite some time to finish this Course, I finally decided to do it out of my own need to find balance in my work. As I mentioned above - balance is the name of the game if we want to live successful lives and have successful businesses.

While you are learning - and working on - the material in *The MASTER COURSE*, you will most likely come to some balance. So, when you begin to see your results, that is the time to find something to do every day to keep you balanced. Most of us are a far cry from becoming "masters." Just when we think we've "got it" - something comes into our world to test us. For me, it was the internet!

This is not meant to be discouraging to any reader in any way. It is simply a reminder we must make using the universal principles a way of life - and not allow *anything* to come between us and them!

And, I might add, since I began seriously rewriting and finishing this Course, everything is once again falling right into place. It's always there. All we have to do is claim it as our own - and use it!

Who, Or What, Is Running Your Life?

Are you creating exactly what you wish for your life? If not, chances are you are operating with core belief feelings telling you – you can't have what you want. For the most part - we are unaware of these feelings.

Who is in your head telling you what's possible for you? Who's driving your bus?

Is it a caretaker from your childhood?

Even though you may know you were taught erroneous beliefs as a child - those very beliefs will continue to color your life. They must be found and dug up - one at a time. Then, examined - and thrown out. Finally, they must be replaced! Knowing about it - and doing something about it - are two very different things.

Is it old habits?

Some habits are so ingrained we cease to be aware of them. We just function on auto-pilot. Upon examination, you'll find some of your operative feelings are no longer valid. You've merely failed to change the habit. Yes - feelings can become habits. Since feelings create, you may be creating from habit rather than from true intent.

Is it someone in your life today?

Are you co-existing with someone who is so self-involved everything in your life must revolve around them - and what they want? Have you bought into the idea that your desires should always come last? Is it always about them - and never about you? Have you allowed someone else to determine where you're going - or not going?

Is it the need for relationship?

If you are driven by the need to be involved in an intimate relationship, you're not feeling fulfilled as an individual. Good relationships come about when the relationship is wanted - not needed. If you feel life won't be complete without the perfect relationship, you're setting yourself up to fail in everything you try on your own.

Is it lack of self-esteem?

If so, better find out where that picture of yourself developed. And, get rid of it! You cannot rebuild your ideas of yourself - and what's possible for you - until you find and redraw what has been painted for you.

So ... Do you know who's driving your bus through life? Do you know what do to about it if it isn't you? Is it time for you to take the wheel?

Change your core belief feelings and you will change what you create for your life. Use the self-analysis guide, *"Who's Driving Your Bus?"* It has been included as the Appendix of this course to function as your workbook. *It's your most powerful tool for transformation!*

Additional Resource

My goal is to bring *The MASTER COURSE* material to as many people as possible - at the lowest cost possible. You can find a multitude of very high-priced seminars which will give you the information - then leave you to work it out on your own, with no ongoing support.

All techniques used in this Course are explained using the basis of the principles involved. This not only increases your success ratio, it ensures your desired changes move on toward complete - and lasting - transformation.

The MASTER COURSE Workbook, *"Who's Driving Your Bus?"* is a Self-Analysis Guide to help you uncover your personal core belief feelings in a gentle and safe manner. It includes instructions for changing fear feelings into the more positive feelings necessary to creating your own personal desires. It's of utmost importance to find all core beliefs that can sabotage your success with creative techniques.

I used this same material in my spiritual therapy sessions with great success. At the outset, very few people have any idea of the number of fear beliefs they hold which are creating for them exactly what they do not want. The Self-Analysis Guide will help you find those fears - and remove them.

This Workbook is included in *The MASTER COURSE* package at no extra cost to you!

I look forward to receiving a letter from you, telling me about your successes. Even though I get an enormous amount of mail, keep the letters coming. I love to hear your success stories!

Appendix

Self-Analysis Guide

This personal self-analysis guide is the workbook for *The MASTER COURSE*. It is used throughout the entire Course, and it's very important you do the exercises as completely as possible.

People wishing to make positive changes in their lives use many techniques. Creative Visualization - Affirmations - Meditation - Motivational Training - and various other processes. All of these techniques work!

Problem is - they only work for some of the people, some of the time. Or they work for a while - then begin to fall apart with time. We tend to forget we are constantly creating our own life situations - or accepting certain situations in our lives - without being aware of it. Everything that goes on in our lives is created by our feelings!

Our feelings set up certain vibrational energies. These energies go out into the universe and meet with complementary energies. Then, they begin to create the situations that lie behind the feeling.

It seems it should be a simple thing to control what feelings we send into the universe. We can - once we're aware of them - but many of our most powerful feelings are buried in our unconscious minds, completely out of our awareness.

The unconscious mind is a giant automatic memory bank. It's neither good nor evil. Everything is stored there - every life memory - all cell memory - and most importantly, the feelings we connect to each memory. It allows us to do things automatically, without needing to think about it. It also causes us to respond automatically when certain situations trigger unconscious feelings.

When problems arise, it's because we have been taught certain - usually incorrect - concepts that create deep feelings within us. It's these feelings that automatically control our responses, causing certain actions - or reactions - on our part. These feelings - whether we acknowledge them or not - actually determine what we attract into our lives.

We can remember anything we choose to remember if we use the proper techniques. But, why clutter up our conscious minds with all that information? We don't really need it unless we want to change a habit, or some other type of automatic response, which is causing us problems. Developing new automatic responses will guarantee you can have the life you desire.

Your unconscious mind is completely impartial. It never makes a decision - and, in fact, couldn't if it wanted to - because it doesn't know the difference between what's "real" and what isn't. So what does it do? It blindly accepts everything it sees or hears as true - records any feelings involved - then helps you attract or create situations in your life - based on those feelings.

This unconscious part of the mind can't tell the difference between something you see with your eyes - and something you "see" by imagining it in your mind. Right! An image in your mind is just as true to the unconscious mind as something you visually see "out there."

You already have many pictures in your unconscious and some of them are exact opposites. Which does the unconscious accept? Both! But, which does the subconscious prompt you to act upon? You will only act upon the images with intense feelings surrounding them. These are the memories that become your core beliefs.

All of your core beliefs have been planted - and sustained - in your unconscious mind for years! And you can bet they were planted with feeling! They have become "beliefs," not because someone "taught" you something - but because whatever you were taught had intense feelings surrounding it. Those feelings went out into the universe and created for you exactly what you were taught. *Then*, the belief came into being.

Some type of fear underlies every single negative response pattern that keeps us from creating - or keeping - what we want in life. It may be fear of different things - but its fear nonetheless.

Feeling creates! Not words - not thoughts - not beliefs. Feeling! Emotion! Fear is a powerful emotion!

Only two basic feeling energies exist in reality: fear - and love. Take any emotion you can think of and it will reduce to one of these basic feelings. Anger = fear. Joy = love. Everything falls at one end of the spectrum or the other.

Your feelings have been stored in your unconscious mind. Many have been there for a very long time - creating exactly the circumstances of your life today. Remember - it doesn't have to make sense. The unconscious can't reason. If your life isn't exactly what you'd like it to be - then some of those core belief feelings need to be changed.

Fear is the underlying feeling of core beliefs creating challenging situations. That fear can be transmuted into love. Once this is accomplished, the blocks to your desires are removed. Then, the energy of the love feelings can go out - attracting like energies of love - and begin creating the happiness you desire.

The questions in this self-analysis will help you discover astounding truths about yourself. They will allow you to gently remember how you acquired certain beliefs and analyze why you continue to hold them. You will also learn to identify the creative feelings involved.

Best of all - you'll learn how to replace those belief feelings with something that moves you forward - rather than holding you back!

The result? You will begin attracting - and keeping - the kind of life experiences you always wanted but couldn't accept due to those old programmed feelings: more money - happy relationships - glowing good health. You'll have more - you'll be more - you'll look great!

Directions

First of all – relax! Pay particular attention to the *very first answer* that jumps into your mind as you read each question. Then, take some time to really think about it. Relax! Stay as relaxed as possible to allow old memories to drift up into your conscious mind. Relax!

Copy each question into a notebook - or make a special computer file. Fill your answers in right below each question. Upon first reading, the questions may seem very simple to you. This is part of the system. If you are working correctly, you will find these very simple questions have quite complicated answers.

When you begin to feel stressed over finding the answers (and, you will), walk away from it. Stop trying to remember. You'll find, as you go about your other activities, you'll have sudden memories regarding the questions. Jot them down. Then, when you can, come back to the Guide and type them in. Find as many answers as you can to each question.

Don't try to answer each question completely the first time. Write down the things that come up easily in as much detail as possible. Take your time working through the questions. Once a question is in your mind, the answer will often come to you suddenly while you're doing something else.

Be willing for it to take some time before you have your complete answers. In fact, a year from now you may have a sudden revelation regarding some of these answers. That's okay. By then, you'll know what to do with it right away. In the beginning - don't push yourself.

Don't concern yourself about bringing up negative thoughts and feelings. Everything that's holding you back has a negative thought or feeling attached to it. Do this very objectively. By that, I mean - don't get too involved in any feelings about anything you remember.

Simply look at it with the knowledge that all you're doing is an "inspection" to see where you need to make some changes. Look at the feelings involved with each situation, but don't get caught up in them. Just know - it can be changed.

This is very important! It some sections, you will be asked to list your feelings, and determine if they are fear-based - or love-based. Remember, all negative - or painful feelings - are fear-based.

Search for the underlying fear in every emotion such as anger - envy - resentment - indignation, etc. Define the fear. It is fear of ... what? Then, search your memory until you find where that fear began.

As you search your memories, you will find memories of situations that may make you very angry - or very sad. As this happens, write down all of your feelings - and your thoughts - regarding that situation. Do this on separate pages from your workbook files.

Pour everything onto that paper that you need to get out of your system. Be as hurt, or angry, as you like. Express *everything* in any way that feels right to you. Do it as completely as possible.

The idea is to move those feelings *out* of your being - and onto the paper. You are moving energy. When you have finished with each of those outpourings, put that paper aside. *Do not re-read it!* You'll receive instructions on what to do with it later in this Guide. Remember - these are separate files from your daily workbook. Keep them separate!

This is your personal self-analysis and should be kept completely private!

This entire process could become adulterated very quickly if you are concerned about someone else seeing your answers. Be rigorously honest! And again, give as many answers as you can to each question - even if they don't seem to make sense. Remember - there's nothing rational about your unconscious feelings.

In order for this self-analysis to be valuable to you - you're going to have to do some work. Write down - in detail - everything that comes up as you work through the questions. You can't change something until you can see it needs to be changed - so *write everything down!* Following the questions, you will find suggestions and exercises for transmuting these memory beliefs, and automatic responses, into positive feelings.

Questionnaire

Do not begin answering these questions until you have a thorough understanding of the two paragraphs regarding fear in the preceding directions.

As you work through the questions, remember to write down *all* of your thoughts - *in detail!* Don't concern yourself with what to do with the information at this point. We'll get to that later. First, just search your memory for information.

Ask Yourself:

1. What do you truly believe about yourself?

- Write a description of who you are. This is *not* about an image - or what you would like for others to see in you. Write about what you feel about yourself deep inside. The good - the bad - and the ugly.

- List the feelings that come up as you write this. Alongside each feeling, note whether it is based in love - or fear. Do not get emotionally involved in this - *you're only looking for information!*

2. What do you truly believe is possible for you?

- If your life continues in the same way it's been going, what do you see as the ultimate heights you can accomplish? Project yourself into the future. Write down what you expect to see. Not what you want - but - *what you expect*.

- List the feelings that come up and determine whether they are based in love - or fear.

3. *Where did you get those ideas?*

- Try to list everything that's ever been communicated to you (in any way) that told you what you could expect from life.

- Project yourself back to the time you received a message and write down any feelings you experienced at the time. Those feelings will automatically re-create themselves as you remember. Determine each one to come from love - or fear. Remember, it doesn't have to make sense!

- If the ideas communicated to you were negative as to your possibilities, write down who was with you at the time. Exactly what was said? Who said it? What was the situation of the moment? Was this person angry? Frightened? Was the person making statements based on his or her own experience? Did it really have anything to do with you?

Looking at the major situations in your life today.

4. *What is expressing in your life that you do not want?*

- List all the situations in your life today you would like to *change*. These are only the situations you do *not* want. These can include (but are not limited to) your finances - career - specific relationships, or lack thereof - health and physical attributes - environment - everything!

- Write the main feelings that come up as you think about each situation. Determine each one to be love - or fear.

5. *What do you want that you don't seem to have?*

- Make a "wish list" - be specific. In order to create the things that we want in life, we must be very clear about what they are.

- As you write each one down, you will probably hear some thought in your mind. It may be something that was communicated to you at some time in the past.

1. Write it down right beside the wish.
2. Note the exact words.
3. Note where you first heard that idea
4. Note the feeling and identify it as love - or fear.

Examine your answers to the previous two questions carefully. For now, just accept that situations are either *in* your life - or *not* in your life. Center yourself in the way your life is expressing right now. Then, answer the following questions about your life today.

6. *Did you choose it or was it chosen for you?*

- This is one of those places to be rigorously honest. Even though we always make the final decisions about our lives, often we are doing it to please, pacify, or honor what someone else wants.

- If you find places where you have made decisions based on another's wants or needs, note what feelings come up when you realize that.

7. *Do you believe this is the way your life must be?*

- If you have this belief, write down the reason why you believe it.

- Think about whether or not it's a valid reason. Write your thoughts.

8. *Write down the way you see your life – as it is today – in your mind.*

- Do you picture tomorrow being the same as today?

- When you think about doing something you want to do - do you see it in the same context as life today? For instance: If you think about moving to new living quarters, do you imagine it in the same financial bracket as what you have now? Write down how you see it.

9. *Aside from what you are writing now, do you ever write about your life as it is today?*

- List the places where you write about it. For instance, in letters - poetry - a journal. Be sure to list everything.

- List any people you may write it for, who are only too happy to agree with you. Or, who may be reinforcing it for you.

10. *Do you talk about your life as it is today?*

- List the statements you routinely make such as: "I can't afford it." - "This job is a pain in the neck." - "I can't ..." - "Those kids are out of control." - "I guess I'll just always be fat." Anything you say that states a fact you would like to change.

- *Pay attention on a daily basis and add to your worksheets every generalization or automatic statement you hear yourself make.* This could be a very long list.

11. *Have you unconsciously accepted generalizations as absolute truth?*

    - List the statements you make without actually thinking about them. Such as: "All men/women are _____" - "You have to be ____ to get ahead in this world."

    - Write down things you've accepted without question regardless of their validity. Such as: "All the men in this family have bad hearts." - Or - "I can't lose weight." – "No one in our family has ever been truly successful."

12. *Are you acting as if something cannot be changed?*

    - Take your time with this. See if you have any of the following *types* of reactions - then write down ones that apply to you.

    - You need a new car, but wouldn't even think about going out to look at a new car.

    - You want a promotion but don't believe you will get it, so you do only as much work as absolutely necessary.

    - You have a relationship challenge so you treat it as if it's just a lousy relationship anyway.

    - You're getting older so you excuse certain things in yourself since, "It won't make any difference."

- Write down every situation you can think of where you do - or do not do - *anything* based on the belief that something cannot be changed. List the feelings that come up with all of these types of reactions. Determine whether they are feelings of love - or fear.

Making Life Experiences Work!

By now, you've found nearly *every belief you have that works against you is based in fear.* Some of our beliefs are so common - and have been around so long - we no longer consciously realize fear holds them in place. They are feelings put in place from infancy to adulthood, and beyond. These energies move out - find like energies - then, create and reinforce exactly what we were taught to believe.

It's all too easy to blame parents for every erroneous core belief we hold. Although parents do instill beliefs, many parents would be appalled to find out the unintentional results of some of their words. *Placing blame is counterproductive in the long run.*

Remember - learning doesn't stop when we leave our parents. Anytime something unpleasant happens in our lives, we're very likely to form a new belief - based on the feelings around that situation.

"Well," you ask, "how can I stop that? If I lose something, feel sad (based in fear of loss), will that fear will go out and create more loss?"

The answer is, "Yes!" If you allow the fear to take hold in your unconscious mind, that's exactly what will happen.

Preventing this is simple. *Feel the sadness.* Don't deny your feelings. But then - *let it go!* That's all that's meant by, "working through it."

Deliberately turn your thoughts to finding something good in the situation - even if it's just that you learned a needed lesson. Then, immediately turn your actions toward reinforcing the good lesson. Pay attention!

When you catch yourself thinking fearful thoughts about a situation - Stop! Yes, it is that simple. Turn your thoughts to something positive. Say the word, "Stop!" Say it out loud if you can. Your mind will instantly obey. Then, you can proceed to choose your next thoughts.

I know it's asking a lot. Sometimes events seem so horrible we don't think it possible to find anything positive in them. It's always possible. Many people who have experienced horrific situations take that experience and use it to teach, help, or support others. *That effectively changes the feelings involved from fear to love.*

Changing Core Belief Feelings

Let's review the questions you've answered and see how a change in beliefs can help you. It's much easier than you might think to make the changes. *Nearly all of it is a matter of changing your perception.* Let's start at the top.

1. What do you really believe about yourself?

Beliefs about the self usually come from two places. What others have told us - and judgments we've developed about ourselves.

We can dismiss what others have told us for the most part.

> *Other people's judgments are based in their own fear feelings. It actually has nothing to do with us.*

All children are born with infinite possibilities. An example is the fear of abandonment instilled in us when told we are "less than" what is wanted by the person criticizing us. These fear feelings are hard to shake! It requires a new perception regarding abandonment.

Only one type of abandonment will cause us problems as adults: abandonment of the self. Everyone else may, and possibly will, leave us sooner or later. At the time we may be very sad - but our lives will go on.

If you've been instilled with the feeling you are "less than," you can change that feeling by knowing *you don't have to accept the judgments of others*. Until you sit down and think about Question #1, like most people, you'll probably be unaware of the full image you carry of yourself.

Judgments we make about ourselves are generally influenced by what we consider our failures. Labeling a situation as a "failure" is a judgment in itself. It simply means we didn't get what we wanted. "Failures" can be changed into triumphs by reflecting upon events in our life that have taken place since the so-called "failure."

The universe is inherently good. It doesn't start sending garbage our way unless we ask for it with the energies surrounding our feelings.

Each time we don't get something we want (or think we want) there's a reason. The worst things that ever happen in our lives often turn out to be the best things we could have asked for. After every "failure" something better comes into our life that would not have happened had we gotten what we wanted in the first place.

EXERCISE: Relate the preceding paragraph to your own life. Think about the job you didn't get - or the relationship that fell apart. What came later you could never have experienced if it hadn't been exactly that way? There is no such thing as failure. What we call "failure" is simply an experience that moves us on to something better. And more often than not, we would never have moved without the perceived "failure."

EXERCISE: Spend some time writing down every positive thing you know about yourself. Feel the good feelings involved with that and *accept them*. Every time you start to feel badly about yourself - change the thoughts instantly. Mentally reject those judgments and embrace the person you know you truly are. Begin actively loving yourself!

Always use affirmative statements regarding your positive qualities by using the words, "I AM _____!" Use of the words, "I AM" will further reinforce all of your positive qualities. You will embrace - and embody

- the qualities following the words, "I AM ..." The positive quality following those two words *is* you. Take the time to *deeply* experience the feelings associated with that positive image.

2. *What do you truly believe is possible for you?*

No person can ever accomplish more in any area of life than what they believe it is possible for them to do. This question is, of course, tied to my previous question. If your picture of who you are has been undermined by the judgments of yourself and others, you severely limit your possibilities, albeit, unknowingly.

EXERCISE: As you change your mind's picture of who you truly are, expand your ideas of what is possible for you. Clearly picture all possibilities being available to you as you view yourself as a worthy and successful person. Write them down. Use the affirmative statement, "I AM _____, and I can _____!"

3. *Where did you get those ideas?*

It's good to know exactly where you learned you were less than perfect. Can anyone say a newborn child doesn't have unlimited possibilities? Of course not. Even children born with handicaps have unlimited potential until someone tells them they aren't capable of doing something.

Remember, you were once a newborn child. If you came to believe you were limited in any way - someone put that idea into your mind.

We don't do the following exercise to place blame. It's only for information. It's good to remember: *everyone in this world is doing the very best they can - at any moment in time - based on their own past experiences and beliefs.* You should already be starting to see most of us aren't responsible for our own beliefs. That doesn't happen until we make conscious choices. Many people never do!

EXERCISE: Once again, review the times when it was communicated to you that you are "less than." See each picture in your mind. Now think about why you were receiving that message. Not what was going on with you - but with the others involved? Were the other people involved fearful for you in any way? Were they being judgmental? Were their own frustrations being taken out on you? Either way, it was their stuff - not yours!

Now, allow your feelings that were involved in the situation to transform to gratitude. Gratitude that you are, after all, okay. Nothing anyone says can change what you are. Allow yourself to feel the love for yourself you once felt you were being denied. Give to yourself what you failed to get earlier. If you can't find any other reason to be grateful, feel gratitude that whatever was going on had nothing to do with you in reality.

I should mention here that you might begin to feel anger at others in your life as you begin to realize the beliefs you've taken on about yourself due to someone else's "stuff." Don't deny that anger - go ahead and feel it. But, don't allow yourself to get caught up in it.

Remember that everyone was doing the very best they could (based on their own past experiences and beliefs) - so forgiveness is in order. Anger is another type of fear and will create lots of things for you that you don't need. Do whatever you have to do to forgive.

4. What is expressing in your life that you do not want?

In order to achieve a life transformation, we need more than just creating the situations we want. We must also eliminate the situations we don't want. Again, we need to be very clear about what those situations are.

EXERCISE: Review each situation you listed in #4. Are you sure you don't want it? When you are very clear on this, start listing what you can do about the situation *today*. Never mind what you want others to do. You cannot change anyone but yourself! Nearly every time, the actions and attitudes of others will begin to change as we shift our own actions and attitudes. Consider how much of what you do not want is there due to your own lack of action to change it. Be honest with yourself. Do this with each individual situation.

5. What do you want that you don't seem to have?

As you answered this question, you probably found out the reason you don't have some of the things you want is because someone convinced you it isn't possible for you to have them. That "someone" may be you. The underlying feeling may be nothing more than fear that you can never have what you want.

EXERCISE: Review where you got the idea you should not - or could not - have anything that you desire. Listen very closely. Are the statements you heard in your mind, as you wrote your desires logical? Do they make sense? Decide to toss out all of these beliefs. Then, do it. Replace them with the opposite, truthful, positive statements.

At 40 years old, my husband asked me why I didn't buy a pair of jeans for myself. I instantly answered, "Girls don't wear jeans." I had three teen-aged daughters whom I allowed to wear jeans - and I never felt critical of other women wearing jeans. Yet, it had never occurred to me that it was okay to wear them myself. Why? Because my mother had told me when I was a child - "Girls don't wear jeans." I was still walking around with that belief for myself - even though I didn't believe it for a minute when it came to my own daughters or other women.

I bought my very first pair of jeans the next day. My point is that we may never know what is actually motivating us until we examine our beliefs to see what might be completely irrational. Then we must make a conscious decision to reject what doesn't make sense. It's amazing how the feelings change when we change our thoughts. I've told you this story twice. *It is that important!*

6. Did you choose it or was it chosen for you?

This is fairly self-explanatory and fits right in with the paragraph above. I never chose not to wear jeans. My mother chose for me. When I realized that - I was able to make another choice for myself. This also happens in many very major parts of our lives.

EXERCISE: Once again, review what you have that you do *not* want - and what you want that you haven't manifested yet. If anyone has, in any way, made that choice for you - decide if you wish to make a different choice. You may *not* wish to make a different choice - and that's okay. At least now you know - whatever the choice is - it has become *your* choice. Maybe you'll even decide to change it later.

If you do decide to make different choices - just make the decision. Don't act upon it until you are perfectly comfortable with it. Think about it until the fear feelings that kept you trapped in someone else's choice transmute into the happy (love) feelings that come with freedom. Then - those new feelings will allow you to act on your new choices with positive results.

7. Do you believe this is the way your life has to be?

Sometimes our beliefs are so strong we can't conceive of things being any other way. This is usually because of the power of the training when the belief was first instilled.

EXERCISE: Begin re-training yourself to accept - *no* power is stronger than your own creative mind. You are a sovereign being and you have ultimate control over every aspect of your life. Learn to say, "No. I will no longer accept that." Learn to say, "Yes. I *will* accept what's good for me." This may be very uncomfortable at first. Your old feelings will try to change your mind. Ignore the fear and do it anyway - uncomfortable or not. Soon, the feelings around your new choices will take over and transmute the old fear.

8. How do you see your life, as it is today, in your mind?

If you constantly see your life exactly as it is now - that's exactly the way it will stay. We must put new images into our minds - and keep them there - before there is any chance of change.

EXERCISE: Spend some time mentally moving yourself to a better place. If you're overweight, see yourself standing in front of a mirror with the image of you in the mirror exactly the size you'd like to be. See yourself interacting, with someone in one of your permanent relationships, expressing the love you'd like to experience with that person. Picture yourself driving the vehicle you'd like to own - working in the career position you want.

Remember, your unconscious mind can't tell whether what it sees is outside or inside. As you allow yourself to regularly experience the feelings these mental images evoke, those new feelings will eventually overcome the old programmed fear that you'll never have these things. In your unconscious mind you do have them now.

9. Do you write about your life as it is today? *10. Do you talk about your life as it is today?*

We'll take care of both these questions at the same time since they are both about words. Words are the vehicles of energy. They have no inherent power. It's always the feeling carried by the word that has the power. Words are not to be feared. We often say things with no feeling whatsoever - and those words will *not* go forth to create.

On the other hand, if you're talking - or writing - about something you don't like, you are reinforcing the feelings that will keep it that way. If you don't like it - you are sending that feeling out into the universe on the words. What happens? You create more of exactly what you don't want.

EXERCISE: Pay attention. Listen to yourself constantly. You'll be amazed at how often you are speaking or writing about exactly what you would like to banish from your life. When you find yourself doing it - stop! Write or talk about what you choose to create in your life instead. If you have a friend you play, "Ain't it awful?" with, either explain to your friend what you're trying to do and ask for cooperation - or find another, more positive, friend with whom to spend your time.

I know many "authorities" recommend journaling your feelings - and I can hear them screaming from here. So, I'd better be very clear on this subject.

Journaling is a wonderful way to get blocked feelings up into your conscious mind. In fact, that's basically what you've been doing as you answered these questions. However, bringing them up for investigation - and wallowing in them day after day - are two entirely different things. One is examining them for change - and the other is sending them out to do some mighty dirty work.

You don't ever need to fear your feelings. Even though they can create a lot of things you don't want - feelings are just energy. The trick is to bring the fear feelings into consciousness - acknowledge them - then transmute (change) them into positive (love) feelings. They are transmuted when you change your perspective to a positive position. Find what was good in the situation that caused the fear - and most of all - practice forgiveness.

Journaling happens to be a good activity for this - as long as you *only* use it for finding the feelings and transmuting them. But, if you're using your journal just to whine on paper - get rid of it. Whining will only create more of what you're whining about.

11. Have you unconsciously accepted generalizations as absolute truth?

Some of what we heard repeatedly as we were growing up is still accepted as truth - even though we know it's wrong. Every family seems to have their generalizations. Such as, "Girls don't wear jeans."

There are also a multitude of statements issued through the media that we accept without much question. Some authority issues an edict that eating too many fats - and not enough carbohydrates - is why we're overweight. So, what happens? Five years later, the average American is more overweight than ever. What happened? Out of the fear feelings the original warning evoked, we started cramming down tons of the pasta every day. Any 5th grader can tell you that starch (which is pasta's whole claim to carbohydrate fame) is the most fattening element we can put into our mouths.

EXERCISE: Pay attention to your own words - and the words of others. Make a habit of asking yourself, "Are they true?" You'll find some of the things you say are utter nonsense, implanted in your mind with fear, years ago. If anything you hear from others evokes *any* kind of fear, know someone - or something - is taking your power from you. Dismiss it.

12. Are you acting as if something cannot be changed?

We've accepted a situation as it is, and everything we do is designed to keep it that way. "Well," you say, "It makes no sense to test drive new cars if I can't afford one." Of course it makes sense. It makes *absolute* sense! Until you can see yourself behind the wheel of that new car - and start the positive feeling energies flowing - you can't possibly draw it to you.

Or, we're dealing again with "authority" figures and our acceptance of their truths. "All the Smith men have bad hearts." "Everyone gets feeble-minded as they get older." "(Just about everything) causes cancer." "There's no point in trying to change it." Yikes!

EXERCISE: Find some very small situation you believe can't be changed - and change it. Don't tell yourself you can't do it. Instead, figure out how you can. Remember to change your feelings about it. Instead of allowing fear to tell you it can't be done, consciously feel how happy you'll be when the change is complete. Then do it.

Continue to do this with more and more complicated situations.

Reaching Your Goal

Throughout this Guide on changing your unconscious responses, I've been asking you to think. It's true the unconscious mind is an emotion-based consciousness - and the conscious mind is more rational. So why do we need to do so much thinking to change the unconscious?

We are attempting to change the fear-based feelings of the unconscious to more positive feelings. This is what we have to accomplish if we want to create positive transformation in our lives. Remember, the unconscious mind accepts everything poured into it, but it will not cause us to act on it unless there are intense feelings involved.

Intense feelings must be accepted by the conscious mind before the unconscious accepts them. The unconscious will accept anything it "sees" but it only accepts feelings through your conscious mind.

Things planted as core beliefs are usually accepted when we are quite young - when we tend to accept things as truth without question - and when we feel more than we think. As an adult those same "truths" can be re-examined for validity. If they are based on incorrect information, the beliefs are easily changed - and the fear-feelings banished.

Now, we're going to deal with any separate papers you may have written, as you moved through the questionnaire - the papers where you expressed anger - or sadness - at specific situations. You should have "poured your heart out" on the papers - then set them aside without re-reading them.

When you set those feelings on paper, you were effectively placing them outside yourself. Out of your being - onto the paper. You were directed not to re-read these papers so you wouldn't take those energies back into your being.

When you feel those memories are complete - everything is on paper - you will need to burn the papers. *Do this in a very safe place!* You will be releasing all of those old negative energies back into the universe through the cleansing power of fire.

As you watch them burn, feel any of the residual internal energies you may be holding onto go with them. Release those inharmonious energies once and for all! Allow the universe to relieve you of these burdens. Give thanks - and figuratively walk away from the beliefs - and the pain.

If you simply cannot believe consciously that you'll ever be happy, you can parrot affirmations for happiness 24 hours a day - but you'll never conjure up the feelings to convince your unconscious mind.

Feelings originate in the conscious mind. They are only stored in the unconscious - and sent out from there to create. Therefore, the unconscious mind will not send out the feelings to create your happiness if you can't believe it - and more importantly, feel it - consciously.

This Self-analysis Guide was created to help you re-train yourself to know everything can be changed. If you've worked through all the questions and exercises in depth, you are on your way to transmuting the negative feelings that hold you back into the positive feelings that will create your deepest desires.

It does take a lot of time and attention. It's taken many years to acquire all that negativity. You won't change it overnight. You'll probably still be adding to your lists years from now. But, if you are determined to begin the changes that can transform your life, you will stay committed. Nothing will change without reprogramming your belief systems.

Relaxation

It is imperative you learn and use this technique when creating life transformations. This is the most important exercise you can do. Do it daily!

Meditation has been proven to strengthen the immune system. Learn the most powerful - yet simple - meditation technique to eliminate stress, provide energy, reverse the aging process, and enhance life.

We live in chaotic times. So chaotic, in fact, it's almost impossible to find a way to completely unwind and have stress-free time. Yet, without that time, it's a futile effort to expect to use creative techniques effectively. It's certainly a losing battle trying to gain any real control over your life.

Even the best techniques, and the most thorough knowledge and understanding of your inner self, won't work for you if you can't find a few stress-free moments every day. You must be able to clear your mind in order for transformative techniques to work.

A daily period of quiet meditation is clearly your best shot at relieving stress. It certainly replenishes energy - and can even reverse aging! However, many people insist they are unable to empty their minds of thoughts. I can't tell you how many people I've seen become even more stressed struggling to achieve a meditative state.

What I'm about to teach you is a type of meditation - and it's very simple to do. This technique is also far superior to any other type of meditation.

Not only is it easy - you'll receive immediate benefits. I've found once people learn this technique - they love to do it. That takes care of the, "I don't have time" problem. We make time for things that feel good.

One of the reasons people feel so out of control is they can't stop the "mind-chatter" long enough to get a grip on what they need to do.

Those who attempt most meditative practices become frustrated because - even when they deliberately try - they can't quiet their minds.

Frustration is completely needless because it is impossible to force your mind to go blank. Nature abhors a vacuum. The second your mind should become empty, more thoughts will rush in to fill it. I'm going to give you the technique, then I'll explain why it works - how it works - and what you can expect to gain from it.

Meditation Technique

Do this meditation exercise anywhere you feel comfortable. In the beginning, either sit or lie down. Later, you'll find you'll be able to do it standing in line at the supermarket.

I found this technique, many years ago, in a book on Hindu philosophy. I'll explain it as closely as possible to how I learned it.

For now, just find a quiet, comfortable place - inside or out. Do turn off the TV and all the telephones. If there's an emergency, you'll be able to handle it much easier after 10 minutes of this meditation. Some soft music is acceptable and might even help at first. If you live in an area with lots of traffic, sirens and commotion - don't concern yourself with it. There's no need to tune out all sound.

Close your eyes, stretch your whole body and take a few deep breaths - forcing the air completely out. This is only to help you relax a bit. As you exhale, think about releasing everything keeping you in a state of tension. Blow it right away from you. This is your time and the rest of the world can wait. Feel the freedom in that!

Go ahead and sprawl out, if you like. An upright position, or a straight spine, is completely unnecessary. Allow yourself the feeling of opening your entire physical body to the universe. Become accessible. Think of expanding the very cells of your body. Envision them spreading out and away from each other.

Don't try to empty your mind. Instead, we're going to replace what's going on there. Now, with your eyes closed and your body completely open - you're going to accept a gift from the universe.

In truth, we have universal creative energies coming directly toward us at all times; they are similar to solar rays. They are pure rays of creative energy. This is actually the cosmic life force and it sustains all life. It isn't oxygen per se - it's the energy behind oxygen.

Even though this life force is coming to us at all times - we don't always get the full benefit of it. In order for it to provide us with everything it has to give, we must become aware of it. We must give it our complete attention.

So, as you relax, simply turn your attention to this energy. The easiest way to do this in the beginning is to visualize the energy of light (which it truly is). See it in your mind as beams - or rays - of light shining down upon your body. Feel it as similar to sunbathing. Allow yourself to feel the warmth of this energy as it spreads over your body. Not hot - not burning - just pleasant, soothing warmth.

Again, spread out - open up to receive this energy. Feel it move straight into your body. Feel it moving throughout every cell in your body. Bathe in it. You are now actually breathing this energy in through your cells. Continue to visualize it in whatever way is most comfortable for you.

Don't strain toward this energy. If you try to capture it, it will move away. All you need to do is accept it. The only thing you need to remember is to give this energy your full and complete attention. Attention is the fundamental element of the technique. Feel the energy - accept it. As you do, you'll feel incredible peace begin to flow through you.

If your mind wanders, don't become the least bit distressed about it. Just gently move your attention back to the energy. If you find yourself struggling to "get it" - or begin to feel distressed - stop! Let it go and try again later. Very few people ever struggle with this technique. It quickly becomes something you want to do.

That's it. That's all there is to it! There is no set amount of time you must remain in this activity. You'll "know" when it's time to stop. Until you get used to it, there is the possibility you'll fall asleep.

This happens as the result of the deep relaxation you begin to feel. As you become experienced with the technique, that won't happen - because you no longer need the rest so badly. In the beginning though, it's a good idea to set an alarm clock for the amount of time you plan to spend in meditation. Then you won't become tense worrying about falling off into dreamland.

It's also most effective to do this a couple of times a day. I know - you don't have time. Well, I repeat, you'll come to the place where you will make time. Earlier I mentioned doing this process while you wait in line at the supermarket. As you become proficient with the method, you'll find you can do it anytime - anywhere - with your eyes wide open! It's an incredible, quick energy booster.

"Can't Work - It's Way Too Simple"

I hear this all the time. It always makes me laugh. Just another sign of our times that we think everything must be complicated to be valuable. Life was never intended to be complicated. We are given everything we need to create any kind of life we want - and it's all very simple. Our insistence on making it complicated is exactly what defeats us.

This life energy is coming to us 24 hours a day. It's a great part of what keeps us alive. We fail to receive the full benefits because of our own energy fields. When our personal energy fields are filled with love energy, the universal life energy moves right through it - and expands the love. That's the ideal situation.

Life is so chaotic in our society, however, we're almost constantly in a state of stress. Stress is created by fear energies. When our personal energy field is radiating fear energies, it's more difficult for the universal energy to move through.

The fear acts like a wall - attempting to block out the life energies. Since the energy of love is always stronger than the energy of fear, the universal life energy (which is pure love energy) must transmute (transform) the fear energy before it can give us full benefits.

You may have heard, "Prayer is talking to God - and meditation is listening." Let me share with you an even greater truth. It's been shown by scientific measurement that when people meditate, there is an increase in the positive chemical components of the immune system. When people meditate in groups - this increase is even greater.

Whether or not this is realized, during meditation, one's attention is wholly focused upon universal life energies. During group meditations, not only are we connecting in Oneness with the life force - we are also connecting in Oneness with each other. This magnifies the healing energies, which are always produced with any realization of Oneness.

During prayer, there is a similar experience. When we pray, we are at least giving our attention to some universal power (by whatever name you wish to call it). Yet, part of that attention is focused on the thing we're petitioning for. In meditation, we ask for nothing. We simply receive that which is already ours.

It's unfortunate so many people today are confusing prayer with meditation. True meditation gives total attention to universal energies. The so-called "group meditations" which focus on words being said by one of the participants is not true meditation. This activity serves the purposes of prayer rather than the true purposes of meditation.

According to the Hindu text, the technique I've just given you is called the Pranic Breath. It means breathing Prana (the breath of life) in through the cells. When we practice the Pranic Breath, we consciously give our full attention to the energies of life, thereby, greatly expanding their effect.

Whenever we are in distress - physically or emotionally - we have the energies of death in our energy fields. Fear is an energy of death. Prana heals everything within us we agree to have healed. The energy of life is always stronger. Life energies are always capable of overcoming the negative energies of death.

In the process of healing, Prana actually cleanses aging cells. It rejuvenates and repairs signs of aging. In this manner, Prana restores youth, not only in appearance - but also in condition and strength. However, Prana can't do its job unless we give it our undivided attention. Our undivided attention sets our intent to receive and use these life-giving energies of the universe.

As you practice this technique regularly, your mind will begin to clear. You'll begin receiving the universal (intuitive) ideas, which will help you in your personal life transformation. You'll begin to *know* things. You'll start to recognize your connection to all things. You'll soon be able to realize - and experience - yourself as part of the Oneness of the universe and all life. No matter what other techniques you choose to use for clearing negative energies from your life - the Pranic Breath should always be part of your daily routine.

Epilogue

I seemed to have known much of the information in this book from a very early age. However, I didn't understand it. So I spent years and years studying everything I could get my hands on. Concepts in *The MASTER COURSE* have been gathered from a wealth of information. I have a rather amazing memory, so I sincerely hope I haven't quoted anyone in this book without proper attribution. If I have, please let me know and it will be corrected immediately.

"We Know When We've Dealt With Our 'STUFF' When ..."

This will be your personal guide for measuring how far you've come as you work through the self-analysis section of *The MASTER COURSE*. It lets you see how much progress you've made!

Just send a copy of your sales receipt to my email address (below) and I'll email you a .PDF file containing *"We Know When We've Dealt With Our 'STUFF' When ..." absolutely free!*
jlscott@themastercourse.com

And, please join us on our new Facebook page at:
www.facebook.com/TheMasterCourse

Any and all claims or representations made in this book are to be considered exceptional results achieved by individuals who actually use the information. They are not the average result of everyone who buys the product. This applies especially to those who purchase the information but neither read nor apply it - or, who follow directions only in part.

Nothing in this material is meant to replace medical treatment when necessary. Although the body may heal itself under our direction, medical treatment may help prepare the body for that healing.

* "Who's Driving Your Bus?" is *not* to be used in lieu of psychological counseling for serious mental/emotional issues. If you are experiencing serious conditions from past memories, see a qualified therapist in person.

All information is provided for educational purposes only.

www.ingramcontent.com/pod-product-compliance
Lightning Source LLC
Chambersburg PA
CBHW031308150426
43191CB00005B/127